This book may be kept
FOURTEEN DAYS
A fine will be charged for each
day the book is kept overtime.

JAN 1 8 1982	NOV 4 1991		
JUL 2 0 1982			
JUN 1 8 1984			
DEC 1 5 1987			
JUL 3 1 1991			
SEP 1 2 1991			

A CHILD'S PLACE

Also by Alexandra Stoddard:
STYLE FOR LIVING

. . . *YOU* have a house, piglet, and I have
a house, and they are very good houses.
And Christopher Robin has a house, and Owl
and Kanga and Rabbit have houses, and even
Rabbit's friends and relations have houses
or something, but poor Eeyore has nothing.
So what I've been thinking is: Let's build
him a house.

The House at Pooh Corner
A. A. MILNE

My Special Place

I have a very special place
Where I can go and hide,
And do all the things I'd like to do,
As long as I'm inside.

—NATHANIEL HOLMES BROWN,
Age 11

a Child's Place

How to Create a Living Environment
for Your Child

Alexandra Stoddard

ILLUSTRATED BY MONA MARK

DOUBLEDAY & COMPANY, INC., GARDEN CITY, NEW YORK
1977

DESIGNED BY LAURENCE ALEXANDER

Copyright © 1977 by Alexandra Stoddard
ISBN: 0-385-07939-7
Library of Congress Catalog Card Number 74–33665

To   Dr. Abbas Taheri

Contents

Foreword

You and your child are the reasons I have written this book.

As an interior designer for fourteen years at McMillen, Inc., in New York City, I have come to realize the necessity of a spirited, enriching environment as the background to help a child thrive. I have looked for books by child experts that would give me practical information on how to design an effective environment for a child, but I have been unable to find the help I thought was needed, both as designer and as a parent. So I decided to try to gather helpful information into a book myself. *A Child's Place* is the result. The ideas in this book are based both on my experience as a professional designer and on extensive reading and research into the writings of experts on children.

A Child's Place is a practical, down-to-earth book about how to design a child's room and create an ongoing environment for a child from birth until the child leaves the nest. The goal is to provide a place, a space for living—a place for a child and young person to grow, to live, to be. A place where space, color, and form work to stimulate, delight, and stretch the child's mind and body.

Children's rooms should be set up with many of the same basic elements and flexibility as school classrooms are set up for young children—to encourage industry and creativity.

The book begins by outlining in Part I the constant design elements which will make up this one room, to house the entire growth process: first the question of scale, then on to consider walls and ceilings, floors, windows, lighting, furniture, fabric, color, accessories, maintenance, stimulation, and touch.

Then, each chapter in Part II concerns a specific stage in your child's growth. Different design elements are stressed in each chapter according to what is most important for a child at this particular stage of development. For instance, Chapter 2, "The Cradle," begins the discussion by giving suggestions on how to design the proper room for an infant. Subsequent chapters 3 to 7 show how to adapt this basic environment to suit the child as he grows and develops, up to the age of eighteen.

How to divide up one space to be shared by more than one child is a special design problem that is discussed in Part III. Chapters 8 and 9, in this section, focus on sibling sharing, by showing how to divide a space so that privacy and individual expression are encouraged.

As a designer and mother interested in basic ideas, and things you can afford, I've made general suggestions in each chapter on how to handle the child's place. And then, at the end of chapters, I've added some more radical ideas ("Beyond the Basics") for those who want to try more experimental rooms, tailored to a specific child at a specific period in his or her development.

Appendixes at the end of the book suggest other books to read and places to buy some of the things mentioned in the book.

A Child's Place approaches the environment of a room from the child's scale and view, with an eye toward creating challenges, fun, and stimulation as the child grows up. The book's aim is to show how you can make one room an everything to a child, from birth all the way through the adventure of childhood.

ACKNOWLEDGMENTS

Excerpt from *Now We Are Six* by A. A. Milne, with decorations by Ernest H. Shepard. Copyright, © 1927, by E. P. Dutton & Co., Inc.; renewal © 1955 by A. A. Milne. Reprinted by permission of E. P. Dutton & Co., Inc.

From *The House at Pooh Corner* by A. A. Milne, illustrated by E. H. Shepard. Copyright, 1928, by E. P. Dutton & Co., Inc.; renewal © 1956 by A. A. Milne. Reprinted by permission of E. P. Dutton & Co., Inc.

Excerpt from *The Art Spirit* by Robert Henri. Copyright 1923 by J. B. Lippincott Company. Copyright renewed 1951 by Violet Organ. Reprinted by permission of J. B. Lippincott Company.

Excerpt from *Beast or Angel? Choices That Make Us Human* by René Dubos. Reprinted by permission of Charles Scribner's Sons.

Excerpt from *Yale Alumni Magazine,* April, 1974. Permission granted by Kenneth Keniston, Professor of Psychology at Yale.

Excerpt from "When a Youngster Dreams, It's Part of Growing Up." Dr. Angiola Churchill, Professor of Art and Art Education at New York University. October 24, 1975 issue of the New York *Times,* Copyright © 1975 by the New York Times Company. Reprinted by permission.

Excerpt from "Journey" by Nathaniel Holmes Brown and Sam Ward. Copyright © 1974. Reprinted by permission of the authors.

Excerpt from *The Little Prince* by Antoine de Saint-Exupéry. Reprinted by permission of Harcourt Brace Jovanovich, Inc.

For their indispensable
encouragement and
support, my deep
appreciation to
Carl Brandt and Kate Medina.

Train up a child in the way he should go:
and when he is old, he will not depart from it.

PROVERBS *22:6*

A CHILD'S PLACE

PART I

A Child's Place

Chapter 1

YOUR CHILD'S NEEDS

YOUR CHILD'S NEEDS

From my experience as a decorator and designer (and also as the mother of several children), I've been exposed to many ideas about how to design a room for a child. Every parent wants to create a safe, attractive environment, an environment that will help a child grow into a strong and confident adult, and yet there are limitations imposed by space, time, and money. And, also, the child changes and grows so fast! How can you select furniture for an infant that can be used as the child gets older, grows bigger, and his activities change? How can you design and decorate a room so that it will be personal and yet won't be out of date in a year or less? How can you enrich your child's place with beauty? What do you do about all the equipment that is needed for an infant? A mobile three-year-old? A sixteen-year-old with homework and a special need for privacy? What do you do when it's necessary for siblings to share a room?

This book is based on my experience solving problems like these for many families. The basic philosophy behind the ideas in *A Child's Place* is quite simple: A child's room can be planned from the beginning so that everything for the first twenty years is housed in this one room (although not necessarily all during the same period). Once you set up the basic plan of the room, it should be easy to adapt the room to the child's subsequent stages or growth.

The other primary belief behind the ideas in this book is that a child's room should reflect the individual child as much as possible. Throughout the book I use his and her, he and she, interchangeably, and try to give general advice, as well as specific suggestions, so you can choose what's best for a particular child, sometimes with the child's help.

The child's growth process should be able to evolve through the usual stages, all in this one space. Sizes, colors, and space can be changed according to the child's development and with a minimum of effort and money.

One notion basic to the design ideas in this book is flexibility.

For a child's place to be a growing, flexible environment, as little as possible should be fixed in one place. The room should grow, change, and develop as the child does. The room should be designed for the child, not for the parents. It should reflect as much as possible the child's own ideas, interests, and feelings. It should be a place where you can let your child grow and expand in a supportive world. The room should fit the child and work for him.

The basic requirements are simple. Think of this room as a stage on which some props will stay and others will change. Plan the constants to last; for instance, you'll always have to have a place for the child to sleep, a place to store things such as clothes, art work, and paraphernalia. Free space for creative play, for friends, for books, for important activities, ranging from counting sea shells to having a slumber party. This one room should be flexible so that a child can live out each day in this one wonderful place—"My Room."

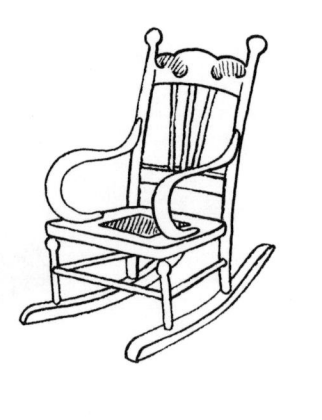

HOW TO APPROACH A CHILD'S ROOM

This book will show you how you can set up a child's room and have it evolve easily over the years, as the child grows up. Once you set up the basic elements of the room (we'll discuss each), the child or children can personalize the rest, and we'll discuss how. Imagination, a plan, and an open mind are needed, not money.

KEY DESIGN ELEMENTS TO KEEP CONSTANTLY IN MIND

There are a number of design elements that you need to keep constantly in mind in planning a child's room. These design elements, or considerations, will exist, in varying degrees, for the child's room throughout the child's life. Keep them in mind from the outset, and adapt them over the years; in this way all your future design planning will be easier. As your child grows, the emphasis will shift among these basic design elements.

The Basic Design Elements Are:

1. *Scale*   The first element to keep in mind in a child's place is scale. As your child's size changes, so does the scale in which he sees things and so should the scale of things in his room.

A museum in Denmark put on an "ego-deflating exhibit" that featured a gigantic breakfast table which dwarfed visitors. The idea of the exhibit was to remind grownups how a child feels in an adult environment. The Danes believe children are not merely undeveloped adults but smaller individuals whose sizes and interests are essential considerations. A child's place should be a total environment in scale and in touch with your child.

As Dr. Spock suggests, crawl on the floor so you can see the room the way your child does. I did this when our first daughter was born and was horrified at what I saw when I looked underneath the secondhand furniture I had just painted. If you paint furniture for your child, be sure to cut the legs off so everything is the right height and be sure to paint the *undersides* of the furniture; that's what the child sees. (I saw dirt, dust, cobwebs, and dried-up chewing gum under our furniture. Right from the start, I flunked Dr. Spock!)

Try always to put yourself in your child's scale, when making design decisions in his room. The next time you walk into his or her room, sit on the floor. Feel the size of an infant's booties, the scale of a six-month-size undershirt. Look at a young boy's truck, or loved-up Snoopy; a child's favorite blanket, baseball bat, bunny; notice the size of a child's sweater. The more familiar you are with your child's world the more you will understand his or her special delights and be able to design to suit them.

Get in scale and keep the scale evolving

Since a child can be made to feel big by having everything in her room fit her size, start when your child is tiny, watch for growth, and adjust the scale as required. For example, the seat of a low chair can be raised as much as four inches by adding a cushion. As we discuss specific age levels later in this book, I'll suggest ways to increase and change proportions without buying new furniture; and, also, in the last chapter, how to make one room work for two.

Furniture and play objects should be of a size that is comfortable to be appreciated by a small child. An antique chest of drawers for storing toys is of diminished value if the drawers are too big and heavy for a child to open and close easily. On the other hand, a diminutive Windsor antique chair could be treasured by the child.

Surprisingly enough, it can be relatively inexpensive and easy to plan your scale (even of furniture) so it can "grow." As I said earlier, treat your child's room like a stage on which the dimensions of the props evolve.

Having things in his scale, day to day, can help a child learn and build confidence. For example, I know one two-year-old who was lucky enough to have his clothes rod placed relatively low, at thirty inches from the floor. He became fascinated with hangers and was able, through trial and error, to learn how to hang up his own clothes by the time he left the crib stage. If you put your child's clothing bar on an adjustable bracket, it can "grow" in height as the child does. To a child, helping himself to his own clothes and putting them back is a treat because it's a sign of being more like an adult; and soon it becomes a habit. Also, proper scale can remove unnecessary frustration.

Another example of how scale can have an important effect on a child: a nineteen-month-old girl was found "reading" one day—with the book upside down—because her books were placed in bookcases that were low enough to be within her reach. Another child, thirteen years old, told me, "I've had this same chest of drawers and these beds since I can remember, but I've always been able to get in and out of bed and use the drawers by myself because they have always been arranged according to my height. *Now* I can arrange them differently." When a child is too little for the height of a mattress on top of a box spring, eliminate the box spring and put the mattress directly on the bed frame over a piece of plywood.

Another way to arrange a bed for a small child is to put the bed parallel against a wall and put a foam rubber or plywood platform in front of the side your child gets in on so he or she won't have to climb too high.

2. *Flexibility*   Keep in mind that because your child is growing (and therefore changing), the design decisions you make should leave room for flexibility. Some designs will only last about six months. Just as the red sneakers you buy today will be outgrown in five months (worn out in three), other things in the room will become outdated. A child's things have a life span that is intense and short.

As behavior patterns change, so should the environment. A revolving room design can be changed as often as you would change a bulletin board. The display shelves that once housed miniature horses and Beatrice Potter rabbits might later display knitting or a rock collection. The Lucite frames that once had pictures of rock singers might later have pictures of the Grand Teton Mountains. The beds that were once parallel are now at right angles, and the shelves in the closet that once were for puzzles and pull toys now store clothing and athletic equipment. Same shelves, same beds, same frames, and same child. One difference: growth. Think of everything in the child's room as being on a pair of roller skates—a flexible arrangement of space and furniture. This room should say yes to possibilities through an adjustable design.

Make things movable. Not only should the furniture be light-weight enough to move around, but also the bigger pieces can be on heavy-duty ball-bearing casters or glides so a child can move things around. Your child should be able to lift small chairs and tables to get them out of the way or to create a new area without asking for an adult's help. Built-in storage pieces, however, do have to be immobile. A built-in bunk bed might save space, but then it will have to stay in one spot indefinitely. In most cases, if you have a choice, I think this inflexibility is a mistake. A better solution than built-in bunk beds might be two single beds that come apart so you can rearrange them if you want.

When your daughter is playing house, she will want to move everything around and turn things upside down. When a new train set arrives, a table or floor space is needed to set it up. Up goes the rug. Off goes the lamp and knickknacks.

When there is a party, or friends come over, furniture should not limit play and fun. Up goes the Murphy bed so there is room for people and play.

Being flexible requires a basic attitude which is receptive to opening up the hidden potential inside your child, through his space. Flexibility of mind and design allow new fun opportunities to be realized and to flower.

3. *Walls and Ceiling* The walls of a child's place are boundaries. Your child throws a ball; it hits a wall. Your child plays with a water gun and the walls get wet. A four-year-old has just discovered a great new way to apply color on paper: spatter painting. Your walls get it, too. A child gets into bed with sticky hands and fingers the wall. He has discovered being upside down is more fun than right side up, and the headstand is accomplished because there is a wall to balance against. Tomorrow's spelling test gets taped to the wall. The latest poster get tacked or taped up. Jumping up and down in bed is no fun without touching the walls. Finger marks and dirt are sure to accumulate on a child's walls. The best solution is a completely scrubbable surface.

Walls and the ceiling of your child's place should be able to be hosed down, figuratively speaking; practically speaking, you should be able to sponge the walls, ceiling, and woodwork with a strong cleaner. How else are you going to clean up the spilled paint, Magic Markers, and dried-up chocolate?

Any ideas you have for a color or pattern on a wall should be translated into a vinyl wallcovering or a completely washable gloss-enamel paint.

Ceilings get Coke-stained, and balls are bounced around and end up making spots on the ceilings. A completely washable ceiling is essential too.

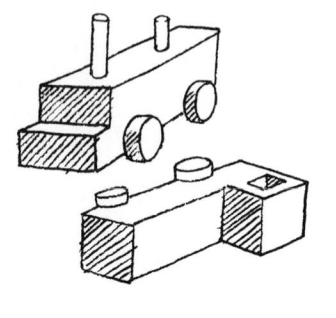

4. *Floor*   Many children have habits that seem somewhat Japanese; they come into the room, take off their shoes, and sit on the floor. Sometimes the most that separates these growing feet from the floor or floor covering are socks which act as dry mops. Your child's floor will be the main surface space for feet, hands, fannies, elbows, tummies, and knees. The floor will be the main surface for building, for trucks and cars, for playing games. Play dough, juice, sand, paint, crayons, chalk, glue, shampoo, cookies, and small spare parts will land on the floor on an average of two per child every minute the room is in use. Trucks and cars, chairs and tables, boxes, broomsticks scrape the floor; and they are dragged, never lifted. Plants are overwatered, dripping water on the floor. Rubber cement dries up and turns dark brown.

When you think of children's floors, think of a hospital's approach to maintenance. A vacuum cleaner isn't enough. Keeping this floor clean requires a pail of hot soapy water and a wet mop.

If you can, choose a kind of a floor that will withstand this kind of beating, at a reasonable cost. Pick one that is easy to maintain.

One of the most practical floors for the early childhood years is a wood or vinyl floor, dressed up with removable area rugs. Wall-to-wall carpeting, with a few exceptions, is expensive, limiting, and a problem to keep clean. Odors accumulate in the carpeting and can't be entirely eliminated by ordinary cleaning. Staining is always a problem with wall-to-wall carpeting because the really bad accidents inevitably land in the most conspicuous places. A chemistry experiment might be a success, but the carpet below may have lost its color. A rug which can be moved around will be preferable in the long run.

If you have a wooden floor in your house or apartment already, by all means leave it there to see and enjoy. In the following chapters, ways to color and stain a wood floor so that it is easy to maintain will be suggested. (Many school gymnasiums still use wood, heavily protected and smooth.)

If you live in a space which does not have a wooden floor, consider putting in an asbestos vinyl tile or a regular vinyl tile floor.

Area rugs over a wood or vinyl floor solve the problem of
warmth and softness, add color, pattern, and texture and still
provide the hard floor surface needed for block building and
train tracks.

5. *Windows*   A window in a child's place connects your child
with the sky, clouds, stars, sun, and a changing view—and brings
in fresh air. Your windows should be clean so they will let in all
the natural light; add guards and locks for safety. One day my
daughter Alexandra was staring at the moving clouds from her
window, and she called to me, "Mommy, quick. Look, the buildings are moving!" Children watch a rainstorm with their noses
pressed to the window. A window connects a room to the out-of-
doors, allows natural elements to be a part of this inside space,
and makes a room live.

6. *Lighting*   A child's place should be filled with as much light
as possible. You may have to supplement natural light with good
strong incandescent (lamp) lighting which is as close to natural
light as you can get. Exaggerate your lighting. If your child is
playing checkers on the floor, the ceiling light has to be that
much more powerful to light up the floor. Have several varied
lighting possibilities for different moods and to supplement daylight and to create smaller areas within a larger space. Lamps get
hot and your child could get burned; so keep this in mind when
you select your lamps and when you decide where they are to go
in the room. Some modern plastic lamps don't get hot. An exposed bulb, even in a closet, might get shattered by a hockey
stick or a flying Frisbee; plan a covering for it, such as a ceiling
can light with a grille on the bottom.

The light you provide will encourage activity. As soon as your
child is able to read, a safe light for reading in bed will be important. Lighting is one of the room elements that will go through a
lot of changes during the child's youth. If you have outlets located on all four walls, you will have greater flexibility in your
lighting later. Extension cords can be dangerous in a child's
room. A light in the ceiling for gloomy winter days is helpful. In
addition, you might add some white horizontal or vertical wall
can lights which wash light up and down and are out of reach
for the child, therefore out of danger.

7. *Furniture*   As discussed earlier, think of furniture as the
movable props on your changing stage, and choose pieces which
can be moved around easily. Children's furniture should be

solidly built and designed for hard use. Furniture, like building blocks, needs to be played with to be appreciated. Furniture should say yes to fun and activity. An antique pine high piece with hinged cupboards below will be used to store toys and, also, the cupboard doors will be sat on and played with, so be sure the hinges are solid. A high piece in a child's place might be bolted against the wall for safety.

I don't recommend spending money on small-size furniture for children. Rather, buy things you can adjust to a child's scale. Except for the purely functional equipment you need for the early years, and the indulgence of an antique piece which will be passed on, furniture should be purchased for the whole childhood period. A client recently showed me metal furniture she had as a child in the thirties. Solid, well-designed, simple, and lasting—this lacquered metal furniture is ageless. The drawers move easily, and there are locks on some of them. What a good investment! There are companies which manufacture furniture in small sizes made of heavy, brightly colored cardboard; far better to spend a small sum on this type of disposable furniture until you are ready to purchase solid furniture that will last. Children get attached to their things, and if the furniture they grow up with is still in one piece, they will keep it around long after they're grown.

8. *Fabrics*   Children are stimulated and comforted by texture and pattern. All materials, whenever possible, should be machine washable. If your daughter gets a bloody nose on her bedspread, will the blood stain "ruin the entire bedspread" and therefore the design of the entire room? Children use fabrics to feel secure. Think of comforting textures and consider building up a collection of sheets, blankets, and covers which will add variety and excitement to this room, the stimulation of change. Fabric is a great way to change the whole feeling and color scheme of a child's room.

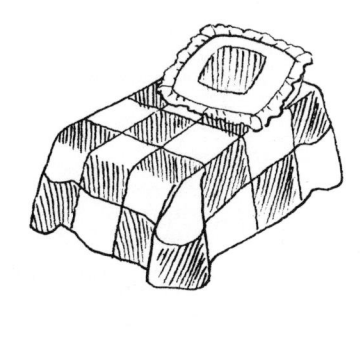

9. *Accessories*   Plan to have lots of storage areas and space because children are born collectors. You can encourage this instinct by having a place for everything. Even little things may be of big importance. Children have a deep appreciation for familiar tiny objects. You should plan to develop surface space for displaying small things and find containers to put things in. This is a fascination in itself, putting things inside things. Cars, dolls, miniatures, beads, scrapbooks, pens—all need a special place. A

toy once treasured might be on display. A doll that once slept in the bed may graduate to a shelf to add color.

The things your child owns and adores will give you all the decorations you need. Create a system to house these treasured possessions.

10. *Color*   Color is the key.

A child's place communicates through color. Color speaks louder than words. You can use color to allow your child self-expression and to expand the imagination of your child. Also, you can use color to reapportion a room. Color will stimulate, uplift, add life, and bring the excitement of change to your child and your child's place. Use color to create a bright, cheerful mood. How much color at what stage? We'll get into that starting in the next chapter.

Children love color. They can take a great deal of color stimulation. In a dark bedroom with no natural light, transform the space into a sunny room by using yellow walls, white trim and ceiling, and paint the doors and baseboard a shiny leaf green. Don't limit color to traditional places. Draw a mural right on a plain wall. Paint a yellow circle in the ceiling or a tree, dripping with delicious red apples, on the closet door. Paint a pink bird flying across the wall or a blue fish under water below. Get out a paint can and brush and bring life into those four walls, through color.

11. *Stimulation*   You can stimulate your child through changes in his or her room, through experiments with colors and design, through textures, through appeal to all the senses. Movable objects—things that grow, change, and reflect—help make your child more aware. The more stimulation you have in this room, the more your son or daughter will understand about the world outside of these four walls. Hang a prism from a clear plastic cord attached to the ceiling window so your child can discover the colors and patterns of fractured light. Hang a piece of stained glass in the window. Hang a map over a cork board and put it near your child's bed. When your child travels to California or Maine or Long Island or New Jersey, put a map of where he or she has been and mark the spot. When the child is older, use pushpins and colored string to show where he or she has traveled and where they're planning to go next.

If you have a light machine, put it in your child's room from time to time. Put in a scale with weights.

12. *Touch*   Sensing space, time, shape, form, textures, depth; sensing reality by determining the quality of surfaces—the squareness, roundness, softness, smoothness, roughness, lightness, and weightiness of objects and materials. All this helps your child to grow in understanding. Everything in his or her room is to be touched and examined. The perfume companies inspired the scratch-and-smell books for beginning readers. Think what sense games you can develop in this child's place. A child touches in order to feel, to understand.

13. *Safety*   Knowing everything in sight is going to be touched, you should plan this room to be as safe and injury-proof as possible. Your child will often walk around in bare feet and if there is a rough wooden floor, trouble lies ahead. It would be wise to sand the floor carefully and put on an extra coat of sealer. Having a safe, childproof room won't limit challenge. On the contrary, if the child's whole world is relatively safe, then action is free to flow.

Inquire from an electrician or your local hardware store about automatic smoke alarms. They are inexpensive and can be installed on the ceiling. Consider flameproofing the fabrics you are going to use in this room. If your child is asthmatic or allergic, be sure you have a complete list from your doctor of the items and materials which could cause breathing difficulties and should therefore be eliminated.

14. *Maintenance*   Keeping this room picked up is bound to be a continuous job. One father returning from work pops his head into his son's room and repeatedly observes: "Frank, did a cyclone strike?" Parents talk to me about maintenance as if they were about to explode. The room gets wrecked every time vigorous play occurs.

It shouldn't be beyond the reach of the child to put his place back in order. After all, if your child can get the blocks out of the box to build a castle, he can put the blocks back too. Any other system assures future sloppy husbands and messy wives. Relative neatness can be an acquired habit, and you can encourage this in your child, through the way his room is planned.

Accidents happen, but if you think about maintenance when you plan the room, you'll be ahead of the game. Magic markers will go through the paper accidentally. However, you won't have to forbid the use of Magic Markers; before buying, test the laminated surface you are considering for a table to be sure the marks can be wiped off. Avoid porous surfaces. Set up a drawing board and a workbench. Have a separate set of cleaning materials in a plastic carryall for each child. Keep a broom and a dustpan in the closet. Why should *you* do it? Make it easy for the child to clean up after play.

Another bit of advice: This is not a doll's house; it should be solid. The furniture will get much harder wear than any you have in the other rooms. Put things in this room, knowing they might break or fall or spill or come unglued, and be ready when it happens. Your child's room will get brutal wear and tear. Ask yourself each time, "Will I be upset if this gets damaged?" Once you decide something goes in this room, you should then be able to live with your decision. Put only those things in the child's place that you think your child will maintain. This learning to care for and maintain things is a big part of growing up.

Put a large wastepaper basket in the child's room for daily maintenance.

I believe a child can be harmed by having someone else do the picking up in his or her room. Teach your child to love and care for his or her own things, through a design and furniture plan that is conducive to self-help.

15. *Privacy* This one room in a true sense may be a child's only real world, his or her one private place on earth. We have come to recognize the importance of the adult's right to be left alone, and it's time to acknowledge as well the growing child's right to, and need for, privacy. A child needs privacy of the mind as well as physical privacy. This can be encouraged through your design plans, even if the room has to be shared with someone else. (See Chapter 8.)

WHAT'S AHEAD

In the next chapters, we'll discuss how to develop a child's room for each of the main periods in a child's life, starting with birth and leading up to when the no-longer-child has left home, with, as we have said, a final chapter devoted to suggestions for a room that is to be shared or divided. The idea is to keep the main elements in mind and design a growing, expanding child's place for your child as he or she grows up.

PART II

How to Make
It Grow

Chapter 2

THE CRADLE

(step one)

The journey of a thousand miles begins with one step.

LAO-TSE
604–531 B.C.

Blessed be the hand that prepares a pleasure for a child, for there is no saying when and where it may bloom forth.

DOUGLAS JERROLD
1803–57

Away in a manger no crib for a bed. . . .

A BABY'S PLACE

Recently I visited a friend to see her new baby. Sarah's older son was at school, her younger son was at home playing with a friend, and Sarah's three-week-old daughter was in a baby carriage in the kitchen. All the confusion of a large family—food being cooked, lunch being eaten, dogs barking, deliveries being made—was amusement for baby Elizabeth. She never cried . . . this beautiful baby girl. She was to live in this baby carriage on wheels for the next three months. To cloister baby Elizabeth, motionless and isolated, on the fourth floor of this large house would have been cruel. Attention and presence are felt immediately at birth.

The material needs for a nursery are so few. Your baby needs you and your feelings of love communicated and shared—love and closeness, touch, plus some food and a clean diaper. There is no real reason for your baby to have a separate room for the first several months. You need a place for some paraphernalia, but not for the baby. A baby is tiny, and the world is much too big at first. Pregnant women instinctively want to "nest," the way birds build nests for their young. But birds don't build separate nests for their babies; on the contrary, a nest is just large enough to fit the newborn under wing. Observe the size of a bird's nest the next time you see one, and then compare the proportion to the scale of your 9-by-11-foot nursery for an under 24-inch foot baby. When your baby is lying down, wouldn't a 9-foot high ceiling seem as high as the moon? A whole separate room at this point in your child's life is unnecessary. If you have the extra room, of course use it. But all you really need at first is a place for your child's things; you needn't disrupt your life by moving, to provide a separate room for a baby, right away.

The assistant minister at my church loved his bachelor apartment. When he married and his wife became pregnant, they didn't panic about their apartment; one of their two bathrooms was easily converted into "baby's place." A window let in light and air, the sink provided running water, and they boarded over the tub with plywood so the bassinet and changing table were the right height for the mother, who is tall. All surfaces were covered with brightly-colored vinyl. The baby slept in her bassinet which was wheeled about from place to place, wherever it was most convenient at the time. Their library remained undisturbed—far more important right then to this family than a spare bathroom.

Your baby needs you, and you need a place for your baby's things. The baby's place now can be where you are; you provide the stimulation, conversation, and companionship he needs. A baby doesn't take up much space; it is the paraphernalia that does. Find space somewhere for your baby's things; at first there aren't too many things needed, so if you find a temporary solution, that's fine. But make a plan that will allow you to keep the baby near you, in a space adjusted to his scale.

Make your living arrangements labor-saving for yourself. A baby sleeps many hours and eats frequently. There is no reason he or she can't be moved around to be where you are. Instead of thinking about space now, think about the content. A baby seat set on a kitchen counter is valuable. A receiving blanket on the living room floor with your son sleeping there is better than your being several rooms away, having to get up frequently to check on him.

Instead of thinking of space for your baby, remember that the need during this period is to give your child lots of fresh air. A baby requires oxygen and nutrients to feed the brain. (The brain of an infant consumes 50 per cent of the total oxygen of the body.) At this time, your baby needs an open window, a park, a yard, and adequate calorie intake.

The Smiths had their four-month-old twins in wicker bassinets in their living room until they found just the right apartment for their new needs. Craig and June were wheeled from here to there, feeling loved each time they were moved. For the parent to have a child on wheels is as convenient as Julia Child's butcher-block work area on casters. Don't limit wheels just to out-of-door use.

A walk-in closet might be used temporarily for the supplies. Or give up part of your breakfast room, dressing room, or extra bathroom, or rig up a storage room you can use for now. You will probably want your newborn near you for sleeping so you can listen with a third ear for noises in the night.

Devoting an entire closet to size six-month undershirts and nightgowns can be a waste of precious space. Remember that at birth babies average no longer than 22 to 23 inches from head to toe. Even children's hangers are too big and get stuck in the small neck opening. Far better to have adjustable shelves and fold the clothes; few things need to be hung up until later on. You can hang something special, like a christening gown, in your own closet before it gets carefully stored away. Even if you have a great deal of free space, a closet is usually inconvenient for everyday changes. You need the clothes piled at hand so your baby doesn't roll off the changing table or off the top of your bureau while you go looking for clothing. Open bins of wicker which swing open and shut are handy and later on make wonderful toy bins. If you want to use a big walk-in closet for storage, why not light it in a way that won't hurt your baby's eyes? And, build in a shelf to be used as a changing shelf which you can cover with foam rubber and a gaily colored vinyl material. This way the diaper piles and necessary utilitarian items are all together and out of sight. Most of the necessary gear for a newborn is not particularly pretty. Show off your child, not your child's place.

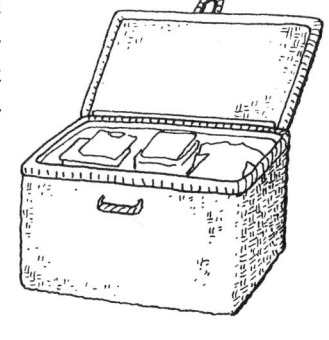

THE NOISE FACTOR

A baby is both noisy, and sensitive to noise. Look for ways to deaden sounds. You might want to install cork insulation if only a thin wall separates your baby's room from the room of someone else in the family.

There is no way a mother (and many fathers) can avoid getting upset at the sound of a baby crying, yet all babies cry, frequently when nothing is wrong. Instead of having to use expensive, thick carpeting and curtains to muffle the noise, plan ahead to see what would be the most intelligent way to help keep down the noise factor. There is a lot to say for peace and quiet, and if an intercom is helpful for checking purposes, consider installing it now. Portable ones are relatively inexpensive.

"LET THERE BE LIGHT"

The most essential element needed for your new baby in terms of a physical space is that it be light and airy. This brings all the goodness of nature into your baby's first months.

The Department of Education and Science published a report suggesting that light from a window provides visual release and also helps avoid an oppressive sense of enclosure, or claustrophobia. So if the room in which you are planning to put your baby is dark, or the window opens onto a dark alley, rethink your space. Could someone else in the family move into that space without upsetting things? Or, might it be better to have your baby go "roomless" now so he can be moved around day and night, thereby being exposed to sunshine and light?

WINDOWS IN CONDITION

Begin your room preparation by getting your windows in good workable condition. I can't emphasize too strongly the essential need for circulation and ventilation for both you and the baby. A fresh, aired room is so important. In cold weather when you don't want to get rained on, you can open your window and bundle your little one up. This can serve the same purpose as taking the baby out. Strip your windows down to the glass and frame and study ways of bringing in maximum light and air so there can be a natural freshness to your child's place. Check now for cracked windowpanes and excessive drafts. Be sure there is a way a window cleaner, or you, can get outside to clean the windows so that both sides of the glass sparkle. Study your window sill and ledge and see if there is a possibility of having a window box installed. Check to be sure your windows are low enough for a small child to see out. If not, you might consider constructing (either now, so it's done, or later) a temporary elevated platform to raise the floor height in your window area.

When your baby is older, like all children he or she will love to sit at the window and look out. Build an insulated window seat now for cozy reading and play times later.

If your child's room doesn't have a window, or if the window gives little light, plan a lighting scheme that will compensate for this.

RADIATORS

Check the radiator. There is no need to have a nervous baby because of a noisy radiator. One mother had to move her baby from a freshly decorated nursery because the radiator thumped so loudly it not only woke the baby up, but also the noise frightened the baby into spitting up and having colic. Even worse, the hissing and spitting noises of the radiator were leaking steam, which can be dangerous. Now is the time to replace your radiators with a more up-to-date-model. If you have an exposed heating pipe, be sure to insulate it or box it with Masonite so it won't burn your child later on. Old, cumbersome radiators can be easily replaced by small, more efficient ones for the fee of an hour of a plumber's time, plus the nominal cost of the radiator. Look into the costs. Estimates are free. Radiator covers can make the radiator safe as well as provide a shelf space. So plan those carefully. You might want to extend the length of the shelf, the width of the window, or the length of the wall. Take advantage of this opportunity to turn a necessary surface area into a useful surface space.

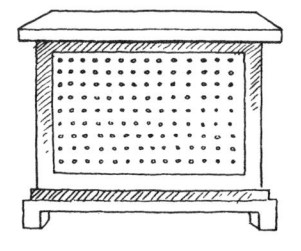

CORNICE HEATING

If you need to install new heating in your child's room, you might look into cornice heating. This puts the source of heat out of a child's reach and keeps the radiator from taking up precious floor space. If you have an electrician doing work in your child's room, you might get an estimate to see how easily the electrical outlets can be moved up onto the wall so they too are out of the reach of a child.

PAINT EARLY

The first design decision is to get the walls of the room ready so you can put a few coats of paint on the walls and ceiling. Do this early on because fresh paint fumes aren't healthy for an expectant mother to breathe when she is in her later months of pregnancy, and they are dangerous to the lungs of a newborn child.

WALLS AND CEILING: NURSERY

The walls and ceiling can be painted with a washable enamel or acrylic paint, or hung with a washable vinyl paper. Keep washability in mind. Plan to pay more for a good washable acrylic or enamel paint so you won't have to repaint as often.

A superior enamel paint I highly recommend for your child's room is a Swedish Emalj paint which comes in four finishes. Emalj is white and it is ground fine so that the paint is smooth, strong, won't yellow, and resists chipping. Painting with Emalj is a joy because it goes on so smoothly. If you are not planning a white room, you can still use Emalj for the trim and the ceiling.

Don't hang a wallcovering you can't sponge and wipe clean with a cleansing solution. A nursery should be the cleanest room in any house and for good reason: children's walls must be able to be washed down and made germfree.

Some parents come to me insisting they want a dainty, sentimental wallcovering for their baby's room. Wallpaper is expensive. But if you finally decide on paper, choose a design printed on a washable vinyl ground with washable pigment. Get a sample of the actual stock "for approval" before you are committed to having it hung, and check to be sure the design or color doesn't rub off.

Nursery Wallcovering   I advise using a wallcovering in the nursery only when your walls are in bad condition. But if you do decide to hang a wallcovering, it needn't have a pattern. The advantages of a wallcovering when your plaster walls are full of cracks is that the wallcovering can help keep the wall together and hide the damage.

The most practical material is a canvas-backed vinyl paper. If you want to add the warmth of texture, hang paper-backed burlap wallcovering; you might even paint it a bright color like white or yellow. The advantage of hanging a burlap wallcovering rather than a synthetic wallcovering such as vinyl is that you can paint over the burlap paper later, whereas painting over vinyl can be risky.

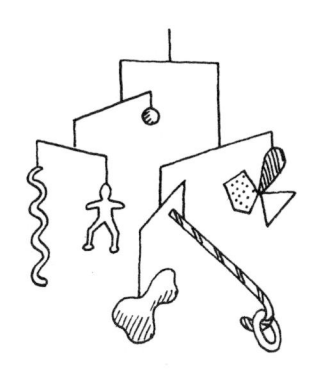

COLOR: NURSERY

Your baby sees and experiences color from the time his or her eyes open. At the beginning, a baby distinguishes contrasts—the bright day after the dark night; then movement; then shape and form.

Dr. Burton L. White, a psychologist and the director of the Harvard Graduate School of Education's Pre-School Project, performed an experiment on the effects of introducing color to five-week-old babies. When the babies were taken out of their featureless white world and placed in a riot of color, it seemed almost too much for them. But at two and a half months the infants were exhilarated by the same surroundings, spent hours staring and pawing at mobiles, trying to feel them. They smiled, vocalized, and laughed.

Start right away from the moment of birth to place the child in a colorful uplifting environment. Experiment with adding colors until you find a balance your child responds to.

Faber Birren, a well-known color consultant, says, "in early childhood color appreciation dominates form appreciation. But understanding the significance color plays in a baby's life, we can expose and give ample opportunity for the young child to live with color, play with color, and fall in love with color."

Wall Colors   When planning your colors for an unknown child-to-be, keep the background yellow or white or a combination of the two. This will give your nursery a fresh, cheerful, sunny look. There is no such thing as too cheerful for a baby's first room. Make the colors fresh and crisp and keep your walls unbusy, light, and simple. A pale yellow with white trim or all white is a good beginning color scheme. You could then stripe the door molding an accent color. Or, if your walls have moldings, you might want to stripe the wall moldings as well. Does the room have a chair rail? Possibly you could paint this yellow and paint the walls above white.

If your child's room is large and gets lots of sun, you might want a pale sky-blue wall with shining white trim. But begin by creating clean lines and be economical with colored walls for this beginning period.

After your son or daughter is born and you see the personality of the baby, you could add colors that seem to fit the child. You will have to interpret what colors are most appropriate for the beginning months, but later you will be able to take clues from the baby. Sex should not determine your color choice, only individuality.

FLOORS: NURSERY

Deciding what to do about your floor comes next. What is on the floor now? If it is wall-to-wall carpeting, my advice is to move that carpeting someplace else.

Is there vinyl on the floor? If it's in good condition, use it, of course. However, if not, pry a crack of the vinyl loose and see if there is a wood floor underneath. If there is, consider ripping the vinyl and using a plain wood floor. Vinyl is okay, but I wouldn't recommend installing it especially; it seems an unnecessary expense at this stage. Wait and see what seems best later. Vinyl is no more practical at this stage than wood, and in many cases it's a lot less attractive. Wood with a rug is the best floor for a baby's room and a child's place.

Wood Floor   Leave your wood floor light in color and put on a polyurethane finish so you can clean it with a wet mop or sponge. You may have your floor scraped and decide to keep it the natural color because the polyurethane darkens the tone several shades. Or, rub a light-colored stain into the wood. White, yellow, or pale green look fresh when rubbed into a natural wood floor. However, if you stain your floor dark red or blue or the usual walnut-brown color, scratches, chips, and specks of dust and dirt will show up more easily. I loved painted floors, but they do chip in time. If you are kind of particular, you had better stick with a plain, stained wood floor.

Carpeting   Most wall-to-wall carpeting that will last and will clean well is too expensive for most of us to install in a baby's or child's room. It isn't practical to put an expensive carpet down because no matter how well it is made it could be ruined in a year if your child is allowed to play freely.

Until recently, there was one exception to this rule. It used to be possible to buy a wool carpeting which was multicolored and didn't show dirt or wear; it was made up of scraps of leftover expensive wool carpeting. The price was $6.00 a square yard, which is extremely reasonable. Unfortunately, it became too popular and the manufacturers ran out of the wool scraps! But if you can find one of these, I recommend it if you plan carpeting.

Area Rugs   If you want carpeting as a blanket of soft cushion underfoot, don't have the carpeting installed wall to wall. With an area rug, you can turn it around or have a good professional cleaner clean it when the inevitable accidents occur. Some children develop allergies and often the doctor requests that the parents remove the rug. If you plan area rugs for this room, they should be small and able to fit into your washing machine and dryer. Your small child crawls around on these rugs and then puts his fingers in his mouth. Dirt clings to toys and this causes bacteria. It should be easy for you to keep these scatter rugs fresh. Cotton (with a rubberized back so it won't slip) is an excellent material for an area rug. However, with the current shortage of natural products, you might have to settle for a synthetic. Choose a rug that is light in color because powder and lint show up more on solid dark colors. Rugs with varying tones of color don't show dirt as much as a monotoned rug. You might, if your room is large, have as many as four or five small rugs in the areas you want covered.

The Noise Factor and Carpeting   Clean bare floors with small washable area rugs are ideal both aesthetically and for practicality. However, noise is an important factor in designing today, especially in children's rooms. If you live in an apartment, you might even be required to cover as much as 80 per cent of your floors with carpeting because of the noise factor. You know your circumstances and should focus on settling your floor problem with as little expense and maintenance as possible. If you are in a position where you have to carpet your floor and you don't know what color to choose, you might, for instance, choose green. Green is the grass, it is nature, it gives you a feeling of the out-of-doors. Green is fresh. A green carpet or rug in a child's room can take some soil and still look okay. Yellow is awfully hard to keep clean; off-white will make your white look cold; gray is a cloudy day; orange can seem harsh, day after day, although that's possibly a personal reaction. Blue is great if it is a real blue, but it shouldn't be pale or all the spots will show up. Pink is difficult to maintain.

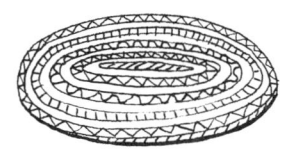

WINDOWS: NURSERY

At the window, you need light control. Some parents blacken an infant's room for sleeping, but I think it's a mistake to start children off with special sleeping habits that will be difficult to carry out throughout their lifetimes. Avoid this, if possible. Also, blacker-than-pitch rooms don't stimulate anything *but* slumber. When you go to an island in the sun, you draw your lightproof drapery across your view of the sea, and you might just as well be in Ohio listening to the roar of cars instead of the pounding surf. And, thinking you are only in Ohio listening to cars, you tend to sleep longer than you need to. Sleep is important to a child's growth, but it shouldn't take over completely. A darkened room is dark enough for most babies and small children to sleep.

Roller Shade or Riviera Blind   You can use a simple lightproof vinyl window roller shade or a Riviera blind which is a contemporary version of a venetian blind—narrow slats and no ugly tapes. For a color accent, you might select blinds that alternate two or more colors. However, since your window frame is white and you will be changing your color scheme as your baby gets older, you would probably be safer to stick with a white shade or blind.

Shutters   Shutters are expensive, so I hesitate to mention them. However, this may be the investment for the windows of your child's room if you want something that will last for years. And if you spend the money to install them now, chances are you will have solved your window problem once and for all. White shutters are charming; they let in light and air and can be adjusted to darken a room for sleeping. If your view is undesirable, shutters give an illusion of a vista beyond and can be permanently closed with the louvers adjusted to allow light to come in. If you have a beautiful view, they will frame it and they can be opened both from the top and the bottom.

LIGHTING: NURSERY

To supplement light, an overhead light is useful, but it should be protected with a clip-on metal shield in order that a strong naked bulb not be exposed. Get on your back and lie on the floor and check to see that there isn't a bulb which would shine right into your baby's eyes. Don't use fluorescent lighting if you can help it; the light it produces is artificial and harsh. Incandescent lamplight is best, and soft light is sufficient at this stage. You need enough light to see to move around; a night light may be a good idea. More expensive lighting isn't important when your child is an infant.

FURNITURE: NURSERY

Walls, floors, windows, and lighting take care of the background space. Next comes furniture.

Every expectant parent would do well to read Thoreau's *Wal-*

den Pond. Don't have your child begin life with expensive things that are unnecessary—for instance, cutesie nursery furniture. Your storage and furniture needs are few; don't purchase a "suite." One of the common mistakes some parents make is to overdo by buying furniture before they know what they actually need—what really will be useful for these first twelve months.

The Baby Carriage   In the beginning it is far better to spend your money on a sturdy baby carriage; this is a piece of useful machinery, and in fact you very likely will soon feel you can not live without it. It must truly be functional. A breakdown while you're out shopping or on a family outing may leave you with three attached wheels, unhinged nerves, and even possibly a bad accident. By all means, buy a good sturdy carriage. And, be practical about your special needs. A huge perambulator might not fit in all elevators, store doors, or aisles, and it can be cumbersome. And, they are more expensive than is necessary for your main purpose, which is to be mobile. You might prefer a folding carriage if you can get a sturdy model. The carriage you select can have a double life if you select one which has a top that lifts off its frame. It can be used as a movable bed for your child for the first two or three months and is wonderful for traveling. A compact, solid, sturdy carriage will reward you daily. If you live in a large house, this carriage can be, as in the case of Sarah, your child's downstairs place. When you are home you can rock your baby in the carriage, and older children can take turns pushing it. (The inside is padded; don't worry.) A carriage is one of the most useful and essential pieces of equipment you'll have until you advance to a stroller—a practical must for night and day use, inside the house and out.

The Stroller   Don't rush into using a stroller; when the baby is in a carriage, you can look at him while you walk along, whereas a stroller only lets you see the top of his head or baby bonnet. The design is motion-oriented, and motion is desired by your baby and helps ease the strain on the busy, on-the-run parent.

Cradle   The next most essential piece of furniture after the carriage, to equip a nursery for your newborn child, is a cradle. A cradle provides a continuation of life inside the womb: For your baby to be comfortable, he has to be comforted, and the good feelings of a rocking cradle are signals of love. Penny's mother, thrilled because she was going to become a grandparent, bought

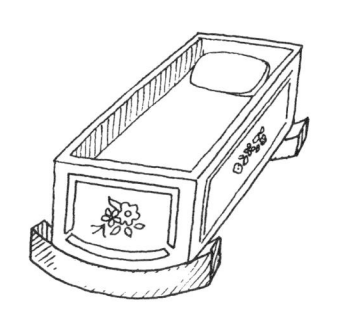

an old cradle in England for the expected first grandchild. A cradle can become a treasure for any family. A ten-year-old now uses the baby cradle she was in as an infant for her dolls.

What are you doing when you provide a place for your baby to sleep? Think what the baby needs to carry on the tactile stimulation he or she experienced in the womb. Deprivation of this, no matter what your good intentions are, is stressful to an infant. You satisfy this need through enfoldment. By supporting, rocking, and covering your baby from all sides, you satisfy this primary need for affectionate, tactile stimulation. Soon you will learn your child's sleeping habits, and you can gradually introduce your baby to the world of more open space—slowly moving toward the larger outside world. But several studies have shown that if this coziness is missed during this stage, your child may later live in fear of open spaces and heights. You teach your child about spatial relations, about closeness, distance, and openness through a keen sensitivity to his need to gradually extend the boundaries of his surrounding world.

I was fascinated to learn that a child who has a preference for bedclothes snugly embracing his body usually prefers his bedroom door closed for sleeping. The child who prefers bedclothes lightly tucked around the bed usually prefers an open door. Your child will let you know what comforts he or she prefers. But at first, babies want closeness. A cradle can provide this.

I have lived with families from many different countries and have been able to observe the different ways in which people live. In my travels I became aware of how people preserve many ancient virtues. The cradle, I believe, is one virtue which should be preserved. And I found the cradle is used everywhere. A cradle, with the infant tucked cozily inside its sheltering surfaces, provides the boundary an infant requires for a secure protective beginning. It also offers the gentle, continuing rocking motion instinctively desired. In a cradle, your baby secures that most important early need of not feeling alone. Remember Newton's Second Law which says that if you actually push against something, something pushes against you. Get back to basics and find an old cradle and swaddling clothes for your newborn child. Because cradles have been out of fashion, you might be lucky enough to find an inexpensive one in a used-furniture store. Or, a friend might lend one to you. Some have been used through the decades by literally hundreds of babies. If you can, acquire your own cradle. There might still be one in your family somewhere. Or, try auctions or antique stores. If you don't have access to a cradle, you could hang heavy rope cording from strong ceiling hooks into the four corners of a wicker basket to create suspension. If you do this, make it reach down near the floor for safety's sake.

Bassinet   A bassinet also makes a good first bed. A canopy top or hood on either a cradle or a bassinet creates a womb-warm feeling. The bassinet serves the same purpose as a cradle and instead of swaying from side to side, you can push the wheels of your bassinet back and forth, to create motion. A baby carriage, a cradle, a bassinet, a lined laundry basket, an apple box, or a bottom drawer are all preferable for a small infant; all are better than a stationary crib. Remember, the need to be soothed by soft touch and restricted by confined space is all-powerful at first.

The Crib   My research indicates that cribs are not ideal for the newborn child. They are too large, flat, and dull, and they expose your baby to a white one-dimensional landscape broken up only by the prisonlike bars of the crib sides. It could be argued that every baby you've ever known started out in a crib, but think again of the millions of babies in other parts of the world who haven't. When your child has outgrown his cradle, but before he or she can move about on his own, why bother with a crib? Instead, you might use a fabric-covered mattress and put it right on the floor. Add some patterned bolster covers to assure safety and reduce the size. (Later, when your child is old enough to sleep in a bed, this same mattress could be used on a bed frame.) If you really wish to use a crib, adjust the scale and proportion of it to the size of your child. For instance, you can adjust the size by covering a piece of foam rubber with material and tying it on the sides of the crib. When you feel you can increase the size, just move the foam rubber down to the next rung, and so on, until your child has grown to the full size of the crib.

The Floor as Furniture   The floor (safe from drafts) is a safe surface for your baby for those times when you aren't there keeping an eye on him. Place a small receiving blanket or old quilt on the floor, with lots of soft, colorful objects and toys around the edges of the blanket; this accomplishes the sense of coziness in an open space, and you don't have to worry unduly about an accident.

Rocking Chair   Another essential piece of furniture, in addition to the carriage and the cradle, is a rocking chair. Rocking soothes the nervous system and has a soothing hypnotic effect.

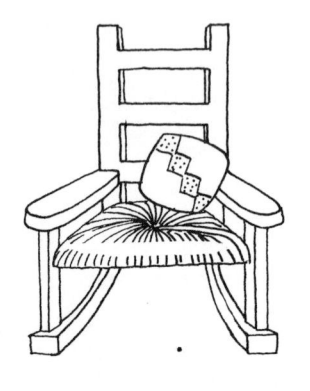

And, it's a wonderful feeling to sit in a rocking chair, slowly rocking, holding your baby warmly in your arms. (Both of you may fall asleep!) In infant-care programs in many hospitals, rocking chairs are provided for nurses.

Doctors often recommend a rocking chair with arms for a nursing mother, as a relaxing pleasant place to nurse a baby. This rocking chair will last for years and can be used by parent and child, so get one you really like. The chair should be comfortable for adults, but this is a question of design, not necessarily of scale. Paint your chair a gay color if it is stained a dark color or is dreary-looking. If you do find an old one and it has a caned seat, you might want to have it reinforced; this chair will get a lot of use! Twelve-year-olds who were raised in a rocker have been known to go and sit in it with a parent now and then. Eventually, your rocker might end up in your family library. Or, it might have so much personal meaning that your child will want it left in his bedroom indefinitely. It is a chair for parents to share. When Dr. Erwin Seale, a well-known metaphysical preacher, retired to a house in St. Croix, he said, "I'm going to sit in my rocking chair overlooking the clear, green translucent water and breathe in the sweet flower-scented air, and after three months, I'm going to rock. Gently!"

TEXTURE

It's important that your nursery should have soft textured materials for your baby to feel. Use color and patterns to stimulate and amuse your child in this premobile stage. Feast their eyes with mobiles and things of interest to expand the intended closeness you've created.

This premobile cradle stage is over all too quickly!

These first months of life are vitally important and there are so many things you can do (from the moment of birth on) to offer your baby environmental enrichment and stimulation. Experiment and find the most stimulating circumstances for your child at each point in his or her level of development. While finding the right "match" and balance for your child, you will try different tools and materials and discover the wonders of the absorbing mind and the eagerness on the part of your child to learn new skills.

Beyond the Basics

Here are some ideas you might want to consider as embellishments on your basic room plan.

1. *Make a texture board.* Cover an 18-inch square wooden board with a colored contact paper. Glue on (or use a staple gun) a piece of fine sandpaper, a swatch of velvet, a feather, some different-colored yarn tufts. Hang it where a baby or young child can touch it.

2. *At the window hang chimes,* a faceted mirror ball, a glass bird, or star. These objects will catch the light and move around, creating designs on other surfaces, and will create prisms of light your baby will try to catch with his hands.

3. *Buy several clear plastic covers,* 8 by 10 inches (with holes, to go in a loose-leaf notebook), put colorful magazine cutouts inside, and attach them to the inside of the cradle with ribbon. Change the pictures often. Buy a plastic-covered loose-leaf notebook to store them; this notebook becomes your child's first picture book.

4. *Make a ring of swatches of cotton material.* If you don't have an assortment of different-textured fabrics in your sewing basket, use odd cloth napkins and sew them on a clear plastic ring. (Eventually they could be used as napkins again!) The more fabric colors and designs the better. Your child will touch the fabrics, chew on the ring. It's a simple, safe toy that communicates texture.

5. *To lower the ceiling height* over the cradle or bassinet, hang a bright-colored panel of free-flowing fabric suspended on nylon thread coming down from the ceiling. Don't pull it tight; allow slack so it has folds and ripples.

6. *Always have one fresh flower* in eye view for your baby to study.

7. *Have a record player* play music.

8. *Light a candle* when you read stories to your baby. Babies are fascinated by the changing light and patterns the candle creates on other objects.

9. *Hang fabric dolls* in bright patterns over the bassinet. When the crib moves, they dance. The child can reach for them with his toes.

10. *Make colorful wool tassels* to hang from a music box. As the music plays, the tassels bob around. When the music stops, they stop moving but add stimulation.

11. *Hang a miniature umbrella* (open from its handle) from a sturdy U-ceiling hook with heavy-duty nylon wire. Saw off the pointed end. The umbrella will move gently and, to an infant, is as thrilling as a moving carrousel is to a five-year-old.

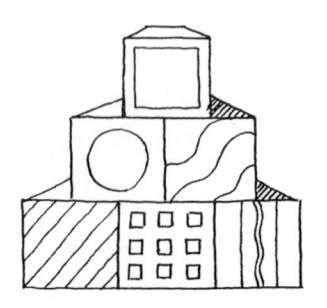

12. *Save all your colored boxes*—the more unusual the shape, the better. Stack them in a variety of ways; change them around often. The baby will begin to recognize the differences. Soon, he or she will want to create these changes. When the child is old enough to play with these, an adult must supervise to keep the boxes out of mouth.

13. *Blow up a baby picture,* poster size, and put it on the ceiling over the bassinet.

14. *Play a tape recording* to your child of her own noises!

15. *Hang wallpaper samples* on the wall near the bassinet. Change them often.

16. *Show family slides* in your baby's room. If you have a slide projector, make a point of photographing familiar objects and show them repeatedly. Especially show slides of the baby in his room.

Chapter 3

FROM CRIB TO BED
(eight months to
three years)

You cannot teach a child to take care of himself unless
you will let him try to take care of himself. He will make
mistakes; and out of these mistakes will come his wisdom.

HENRY WARD BEECHER

. . . We want children to have the richness of
themselves before their eyes. . . .

DR. ANGIOLA CHURCHILL
Professor of Art and Art Education at
New York University

Man is a growing animal, and his birthright is
development.

ANON.

A TOTAL ENVIRONMENT

You will sense and feel when your infant needs a larger world. An active period comes next, when a baby becomes more and more mobile, more and more a person, full of energy, growing and insatiably learning and developing. His space should change to meet these new needs. A baby's striving toward self-sufficiency should be encouraged through designs which allow a child safe exploration in a territory where experiment is rewarded.

Dr. White is convinced that a child's experiences during the first three years of life directly determine how competent he will be later on. The critical learning time is between the ages of eight months and eighteen months. In his book *The First Three Years of Life,* White says that eight months to thirty-six months is the "major education initiative" period.

This is also the most dangerous time for a baby. Key roles parents can play during this period are as designers and organizers of a child's physical environment—one that is safe and encourages movement and activities.

An English nursery-school teacher whom I highly respect once observed, "It isn't important what is in the room of the child at this age, as much as what goes on in the room, which is created by the child." A bright, uncluttered space with a few familiar objects such as wooden building blocks, a ball, a foam rubber cube, a mat, and a favorite stuffed animal or a treasured blanket might be all that is needed to stimulate a child for hours of fun and fantasy. The room, at this stage more than any other growth period, should stimulate and encourage industry and activity; safety is a prerequisite. All the furniture—during this period in particular—should have a purpose.

A SENSE OF PLACE

In the preceding chapter the point was made that your newborn baby is relatively easy to transport. Infants can be taken to restaurants, out on shopping sprees, on weekend trips, and in airplanes. As babies get older, however, the need to nest and "be at home" in their own room seems to become stronger. A year-old child has a sense of, and needs, a place. Space is definitely needed. The room you provide has to function as a whole setting. Your child's room is about to become a total environment within the larger world of the rest of the family. The total space should be utilized as a total child's place.

A PLACE OF ONE'S OWN

By eight months or a year your mobile child has developed a frame of reference. Children learn rapidly and can recognize familiar objects; they become attached to their playthings at a very early age. At this age a child wants to sleep in her own crib or bed; the security of landmarks is important, as roots. When some infants are away from home—even when they are with their parents—they have trouble sleeping and eating. We once took our eleven-month-old on a vacation and she cried for seven days. I was so worried I finally took her to a nurse, thinking she might be teething. Nothing at all was wrong with her but the need to be in her own bed, in her own familiar place. Once home, we put her to bed; she hugged her pillow and slept for hours.

PHYSICAL SPACE

Space communicates with each child differently; two children will see the same thing differently. Plan to organize your child's room so it becomes health-provoking in its richness of possibilities. Think about the quality of the physical space. As you plan, ask yourself if your ideas encourage your child to select his or her own activities. Is there plenty to do to keep the child interested? Is there a good balance between empty space and things in the space which stimulate activity? Too large an empty space is likely to frighten a child. On the other hand, a space completely cluttered with stuff might discourage a child. ("Where do I begin?")

One little boy spent all afternoon putting his Christmas presents away in his room, and he got grumpier and grumpier. His parents didn't appreciate this attitude, not realizing that the new puzzles, games, blocks, and gadgets, on top of all the other things already in the child's room, made him feel threatened. Three-year-old Howard was wondering how he was ever going to live long enough to play all the games, do all the puzzles; and he feared the room would always be junky.

One clever father, at Christmastime, gave his two-year-old son
a batch of heavy half-inch-thick Homasote cardboard sheets
which he had painted in lively primary poster colors. At the
time, this present might not have seemed like much to his son;
however, out of these huge sheets of plywood, his father created
flexible partitions and made a "fun house," a labyrinth from one
end of the room to the other. The four walls of Bobby's place
came alive with different planes and shapes, colors and forms,
making an architectural total environment. Homasote is a recy-
cled product which is a good sound absorber. I recommend
Homasote over Masonite if you eventually want to use pushpins
to add art work and maps. This kind of play with space has a
magical power, and even by doing something less elaborate, you
can create interesting variety within the space.

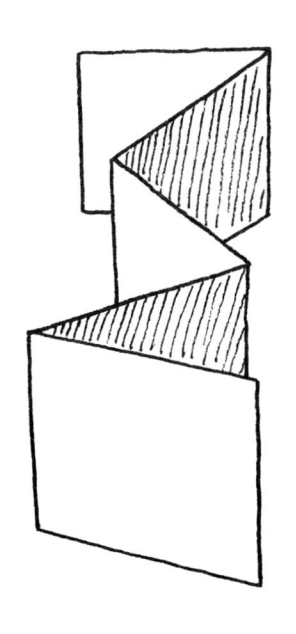

SPACE TO MOVE AROUND

No activity is possible without space. You know how active your
child is and therefore how much space, and what kind, he or she
will thrive on. If you have an extremely active son, you may
need to clear as wide a path as possible for his energy. If you
have a room filled to the brim with toys and furniture, he won't
have any place to play and putter. If you put things around, be
sure they can be used in different ways. Remember to think of
scale and durability. Question whether enough of the contents of
this space will stimulate curiosity. Will your son have fun using
the things in his place, in creative ways? As much as possible,
keep out of a child's room things that don't put a child's imagination, scale, and growth first.

PLAYING ADULT

Very early on, many children begin to play by imitating adult
work. You might want to get a small-scale mop, dustpan and
brush, and a rubber tote with a handle to hold supplies so he or
she can begin to contribute to the upkeep of his own place. Let a
child learn that work can be fun. If drawers are a cinch to open
and close, if there is a simple system of order geared to a child's
ability, and if there is a spirit of fun and adventure, a child will

begin to learn about cleaning up after play and about doing things independently.

SAFE TO YOUR CHILD'S TEST

Your child wants to learn to do new things. The emphasis, from the time your child crawls and begins to walk, is on the development of your child's *personal* skills. As you plan and design this room, try and get inside your child's head and heart. If you grab at a table and find it has a sharp edge, or if in an attempt to push yourself up, you find a sharp edge could cut your forehead, remove this dangerous table. A chrome chair with sharp points on the back could cause a serious accident. If you have a high piece of furniture for display or storage that you feel could possibly topple over, bolt it securely to the wall. (These things are obvious, but make a thorough check, from a child's scale.) Check whether you have a table leg that is loose and if so, get it fixed. If you have a chair that is rough and could splinter, remove it. Take your hand and run it along the underpart of tables and drawers. Manufacturers don't finish areas that don't show, yet those areas must be smooth in order to be safe. Don't wait to discover these things from painful personal experience. Lower the coat hook now—so it is in reach of your child—before he falls off a chair and cuts his lip while trying to hang up his own jacket. Get a sturdy stool for the bathroom with rubber steps and rubber domes on the bottom of four solid legs.

To avoid accidents, get on your knees and try and reach the sink to brush your teeth. Figure out whether a small child will be able to get onto the toilet seat alone without a footstool.

Put guards on the windows. The most attractive window guards are glass (shatterproof) or clear plexiglass bars which fit into metal sleeves on either end of the window sill. In the hardware store you can buy stops for the windows so a child can't open the window high enough for it to be dangerous. These window stops are designed so adults can open and close the window freely, yet a child cannot. They also come with locks. If you paint them the color of the trim, they aren't noticeable.

If you live in a city where, for security purposes, you feel you need metal bars, paint them a bright color and they won't seem so cagelike. I've seen these bars painted green, and the overall effect is similar to latticework.

Secure safety by installing locks on doors and drawers in any areas you feel are dangerous or any areas you want out of bounds to your child—in your child's place and throughout the house or apartment.

Be sure the paint you use in your child's place is nontoxic.

The whole idea is to have this entire space child-designed, child-oriented, child-loved. Don't put breakables on high exposed shelves, to tempt the curiosity of a two-year-old; things you don't want touched should be out of sight as well as out of reach. Negative psychology works on children. If you put things up high and say "No, don't touch," you are offering a challenge.

If you can help it, don't store your things in your child's closets on high shelves, for this same reason. If you need to use a baby's closet for your own, lock it up.

Electrical Outlets   Avoid accidents with electrical outlets by having an electrician install the switch up much higher than normal; or better still, install the switch outside the door. Eliminate all exposed electrical wires. Screw a metal plate over exposed outlets until the child is older.

Stairs   A small baby once fit inside your womb. This baby, now at the crawling stage, still has a way of being able to wedge itself into tiny places—such as between the spindles of a stair bannister. A gate at the top of the stairs is a good idea, but it often may not be enough.

To make the bannister more safe, you could install plexiglass on the front of the spindles. Or, if you don't mind blocking out some light, you can wrap a piece of plywood with a colorful laminated piece of cotton and block in the spindles altogether. If you're feeling artistic, paint a lively mural on the plywood, using nontoxic enamel paint in primary colors.

Another way to block in the bannister is by attaching carpet runners on both sides of the bannister, preferably carpets that match the stair runner or hall carpeting. Or, if you want to keep the bannister more open in appearance, you could weave heavy roping between the spindles, six inches apart. (Safety first and then aesthetics!)

Another solution is to tack simple crossboards of two-inch flat molding onto your spindles; if you space them six inches apart with brads (thin tapering nails), it's the simplest, best solution temporarily, and it is easy and inexpensive.

COLOR

Color is a major element that really comes into play once the child is eight months old. Before the child can speak, color is one of his first languages. By eight months, a child identifies with color, responds to the stimulation, and associates with favorite colors. The most important contribution you can make to your child's developing a love of and sense of the joy of color is to provide fresh, clear, appetizing colors for the room. At this stage, there should be a rainbow of colors for the child to feast on.

The more you vary the colors and combinations surrounding your child, the richer the experience. The Color Research Institute of America advocates changing our colors to suit our moods. New ways of grouping colors create entirely different impressions, and these numerous effects will excite your child. The more colorful experiences your child has, the greater is the potential to use color to create a richer life later on.

All the colors of our surroundings record lasting impressions on us. Color encircles our lives.

Helen Ertel, director at the Institute for National Psychology in Munich, Germany, says: "Colors have a decisive influence on the child's mental performance." The colors that the Institute found to be most beneficial to the child's development are yellow, yellow-green, orange, and light blue. They eliminated red, even though it is popular with children, because red also has the effect of stirring up aggressions.

The Institute researched the effects of a child's environment on his mental growth and found that the color, design, and size of a child's room can have a direct impact.

Children were asked to select colors that would make beautiful rooms in which they would be happy. Simply by pushing a button, an empty room could light up in fifteen different colors. Researchers tested the intelligence of children, their creativity, in the room with their favorite colors and found that a child's IQ rose 23 points in a room that was a color the child found attractive. On the other hand, the IQ's of children in drab rooms, in which they didn't feel well, dropped a staggering 20 to 30 points! Dark, dull rooms made them "lazy and inert." Color can awaken a sluggish feeling the same way sugar can give instant energy.

A child is capable of expressing color preference as early as one year old. There are lots of ways to determine what colors **your small child likes.**

The most stimulating way is through a child's own art. Both our daughters went to parent-child art classes at the age of two. The children sat on brightly painted chairs at low wooden tables and used one-inch wide brushes and had individual pots of clear, flowing primary colors. The children painted to music. Parents painted at high tables nearby. A child's discovery that sky blue and sun yellow cross over the bridge and create green grass becomes a miracle of their unique creation. Instantly you see their own color expression.

Watch what color blocks your child reaches for. Watch what crayons your son or daughter selects. Place small cakes of different-colored soaps in a basket so at each bath the child can make a fresh selection depending on his mood. Have different-colored sponges in a basket and let the child choose a color. In the five-and-ten store, buy several inexpensive colored washcloths and have them stacked in the bathroom so the child gets to choose. This adds excitement to the everyday event of a bath, and you also can see color patterns and preferences develop.

As soon as your child is old enough to keep from putting nonedible things in his mouth, get several paint swatch books at the paint store. Your child will use this as a toy.

You can buy or make four-inch-square sponge-rubber cubes covered with washable lively colored cotton.

To enrich the child's color discovery, buy from Creative Playthings a tricolored viewer made of three plastic disks in red, blue, and yellow. Go to a card store and buy some colorful, decorated wrapping paper and use it as a wall decoration instead of posters or paintings. You can iron out the folds if you don't buy it by the roll. There is no waste because you can eventually use it to wrap presents. You can also buy shiny wrapping paper (flint paper) which comes in twenty rich lively colors in 20-by-36-inch sheets. At a stationery or art supply store, buy sheets of paper in extraordinarily beautiful colors called Color-aid paper (18 by 24 inches). You can tack these sheets onto a bulletin board or tape them directly to your Emalj-painted walls. Change colors often. Add new pictures, or replace old ones, with colorful cutouts from last month's magazines.

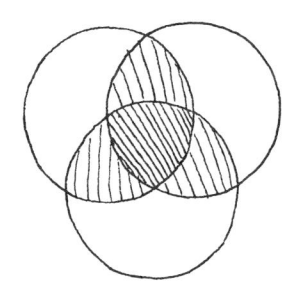

A Bulletin Board for Color   Buy a piece of thin Lucite and two strips of one-inch-square wood the same length as the Lucite. Have the wood notched out the width of the Lucite, so that the Lucite panel can slide back and forth. Install the clear board with headless nails and hang it low on the wall so the child can

use it. If your wall behind is not plain, put a clear sheet of white paper behind the Lucite so there is a plain background to receive colors. You can put child's art on this or you can put colored papers behind the Lucite, and your child can also use a grease pencil or washable Magic Marker on this, to create designs. If you can buy a white metal magnet board, this could also be used as a drawing board for colored crayons, markers, or grease pencils.

Blackboards are fun too, and there are bright-colored chalks available. But the color of the blackboard usually muddies the clarity of the chalk colors.

Once a place that is *safe* is assured, think about the design.

WALLS

The best solution for walls, at the outset, is white or light and scrubbable—either paint or vinyl paper. Young children create colors and images and dreams—their colors, their images, their dreams. With white walls, your child's imagination is free to run wild. Clear colors look best against white. Stare at plain white walls until you have vision or, better yet, until your child has a vision. On one wall you might hang a chalkboard or feltboard with colored felt shapes where your child is allowed to create. Both are now available in standard size with frames and in interesting colors.

Painted Shapes on the Walls   Your ceiling and walls might eventually have a colored shape painted on them for amusement. For example, paint a free-flowing S-curve seven inches wide, on one wall; continue with another S-curve, seven inches wide, on the ceiling and carry this one down on the opposite, adjoining wall—maybe in yellow.

Or, paint a continuing S-curve on three surfaces in three different colors. Start with red, move to orange on the ceiling, and end with a yellow wall. Your child will respond to the moving optical effects color can make against a plain light background. If you have moldings separating your wall from your ceiling, you can paint right through the moldings. Half a circle or square or triangle could be on your child's ceiling and the other half, painted a contrasting color, could be on one wall. *Voilà*—Salvador Dali!

Here's another trick with walls: Paint four squares, in primary colors and with hard-edged corners, about 12 inches square. Paint one on the ceiling, one on each of three walls; you might place them at odd angles, or in unexpected places. Paint in the middle of one a number 1. Or add a letter A. Put a circle in one of the squares. The idea is to use your four walls and your ceiling as spaces to excite, to stimulate, and to educate. And to change.

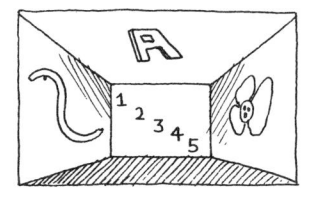

Experiments can be fun, but clean, uncluttered wall space is also wonderful.

Door Accent   If your walls are white or a light color, you might accent the doors by painting each one a primary color. Your door trim could be red, blue, or a bright yellow shiny enamel. Paint one color on all your trim, to frame the crisp white walls.

FLOORS

The floor is one of the most important places in a child's place during both this period and the one to follow. The floor is where a baby is most active, as is the young child. Also, the floor gives you another opportunity for colorful designs and inexpensive, imaginative ideas. Let loose your talent for whimsey on this landing strip.

First, down on your hands and knees again and examine the floor from the same close vantage point your child does. This floor is his turf. Let your mind create all the ideas you can think of as to how you might liven it up, inexpensively. No area of a child's place gets more wear or requires more maintenance; for this reason, I think it's a mistake to spend a lot of money on floor covering. Also, a carpeted floor can inhibit certain kinds of play, in this and the following period.

Wood Floors   As discussed earlier, there is nothing more practical or beautiful for a floor than wood at this stage. Wood wears well and many houses and apartments have existing hardwood floors. Use them.

Your small child needs a hard, firm surface to build blocks on and to get a firm footing. Carpeting causes castles to crash and can look dreadful in no time. It also restricts creative play because one has to worry about spills on the carpet.

Paint or Stain   It is now possible to stain wood floors in a variety of premixed colors; you can buy them at your local hardware or paint store, and, although stains aren't as bright as paint, they are practical as well as colorful. Seal your floor after you stain by applying several coats of clear polyurethane for a waterproof finish. If you have a very sunny room, these colored stains do bleach out, so stain your floor a little darker and brighter than you want it to appear.

Other alternatives, such as vinyl floors, are discussed in the next chapter, when the floor becomes even more important in a child's place.

Fun on All Fours   Because the floor is seen while your child is on all fours, why not have some fun? Wouldn't your child love to stare at his image while he's crawling around? At paint stores and art supply stores, you can buy adhesive-backed silver Mylar paper, to make a distorted mirror that won't break. Cut out a big circle and press it down until it is smooth.

One couple made several Mylar shapes for the yellow floor in their child's room. They had so much fun doing it that they used the leftover Mylar in the bathroom, repeating their efforts on the ceiling.

Another whimsical floor I've seen is a wood floor with a yellow-brick path zigzagging around. This wood floor was scraped and then the pathway was painted on with yellow enamel floor paint, and the whole thing was coated with polyurethane.

One clever mother painted, in the middle of her son's room, twelve-inch squares in red, blue, yellow, green, orange, and white. She measured and masked the squares before she painted them, making the painting job relatively uncomplicated. The effect this floor design had was to suggest automatically a system of order. Jimmy sorted out his yellow toys and put them on his yellow square, his red train was placed on the red square, and so forth. Use a hard enamel paint, and if you are especially pleased with your results, you should preserve it with a few coats of polyurethane which will act as a protective seal. Painting designs on a floor doesn't take great artistic talent since you don't have to be terribly exacting. The patchwork painted squares ended up having an organization purpose, but the incentive which motivated this parent was an aesthetic decoration she could easily achieve herself.

ANOTHER WORD ABOUT COLOR

The moment color enters your child's life you are teaching him or her a language. Your child can learn about relationships, can identify, and might eventually be taught to learn how to read through color symbols. Never underestimate color and its importance.

WINDOWS

Your windows can function as a part-time baby sitter because your child will be eager to see every movement outdoors; children are fascinated by the most minute details. Be sure you have clean windows for your child to look out. If you have a totally blank window which provides no light, and a view you would just as soon avoid, install a white vinyl "no-lite" roller shade to hide the window glass. Then install fluorescent "daylight" strip lighting (the same kind you've seen in kitchens under the upper cabinets to light up the counter area). Install one light unit on top of your window, one on the left side, and one on the right side. (They come in stock sizes.) In order to hide these functional light strips, install a four-inch-wide metal strip (painted to match the trim color on the room) the length of the three lighting fixtures. This shield will box in the lights and conceal the fluorescent bulbs.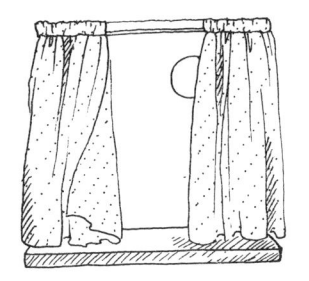

One of my clients, who had a baby girl, hung crisp white dotted swiss curtains across her blank-lighted windows which gave the illusion of sunlight flooding inside. Another client hung white shutters in front of the light strips which also gave the feeling that there was a sunny view beyond. Don't spend much money on curtains because they have to be changed too often to be a practical investment. Hang some whimsical sheets which match the crib cover; then you could easily change them or use the sheets later in other ways. A curtain today, a shower curtain tomorrow, and a sheet after that.

LIGHTING

A ceiling outlet can be valuable. Sometimes old houses and apartments have funny-looking old fixtures which, if painted a bright color, can be fun and enhance the room's color scheme. You might use Duralite round bulbs to replace dim candelabra bulbs. Or, if you don't already have a fixture, consider installing a down can light with a grille to cover the bottom; then a ball can't shatter the bulb.

Night Lights   Studies have shown that many children fear the dark. I'm not an expert on child psychology, but I feel every mother has to judge whether a night light is wise for her child, or whether a hall light or other source of light is more appropriate. Your child may quickly voice his opinion, and you can take it from there! A little light while sleeping might be a comfort and also a safety measure.

FURNITURE

Safe furniture which is easily movable and can be cleaned in part by your child should be one goal.

Crib   A crib is necessary after a child is eight months old; he needs to have regular sleeping habits in a familiar, confined area from which, for his safety, there is no escape. The room outside of the crib should be furnished with objects your child can easily manage; otherwise you are creating a safe environment only as big as the length and width of the crib. Your child will probably remain in the crib for a good portion of this stage, graduating into a bed at about two years old.

I don't advise spending money on a special youth bed with crib sides. As soon as your child is able to walk and begins to know something about toilet training, he can go into a standard-size single bed, so I don't recommend beds that don't use stand-ard-size sheets and standard-size department store bedding. And don't spend a lot of money on the crib, it's an item that will be used for such a short period of time. Maybe you can share this expense by borrowing a crib from a relative or friend. Plan now for growth.

If you can, position the crib, or the bed with rails, near a win-dow (after checking for drafts) so naps and presleep time can be spent gazing out. When it gets light later in the day, this can prove to be an important time to have the bed in range of a view.

When a Child Leaves the Crib   Each child graduates from a crib to a bed at a different age; the rambunctious son of a friend of mine kept climbing over the crib sides, so a bed was the solution for him, at twenty months. It's not a good idea to confine a child in a crib once he's really outgrown it. Most standard American cribs (30 by 54 inches overall, 27 by 51- or 52-inch mattress size) are quite large, so when it is the proper time to leave the crib and move into a bed, the standard single bed won't seem too big.

Youth Beds   The theory behind youth beds is that you shouldn't shock the child by taking him out of a small, cozy place and thrust him into a big, unfamiliar bed. However, I feel there are other ways of getting around this problem without spending money on a transitional bed, one that will have a relatively short life. If you have a neighbor who has a youth bed you can borrow, that's one thing. However, many youth beds are the exact size of a standard American crib. Scandinavian Imports has an adjustable youth bed that is 30 by 54 inches long and can be extended to 87 inches long. The mattress cover is larger than the mattress, so you can add a piece of foam rubber to the end to make it grow. But then you are stuck with a very odd-size mattress and no standard bedding to fit it properly. Because a youth bed is so close in size to the American-size crib, I personally feel this transient piece of equipment is unnecessary.

Side Rails   For the first few weeks the child is in a big bed, after being in a crib, you might want to add nylon-mesh side rails for added safety. They are inexpensive and can be purchased at most department stores.

Beds   You may have started your baby in a laundry basket, cradle, or portable carry tote, then moved to a carriage. Then, if it was convenient, your child may have slept in a crib until he or she was old enough to stay put. Or, when he was able to walk, get up and go to the bathroom alone. From this "standard" crib, your child will probably advance to a "standard" single bed (anywhere from 30 to 39 inches wide by 70 to 80 inches long). However, few things are "standard," as you can tell from this range of widths and lengths, because many designs are now available in America from Scandinavia, Germany, Poland, France, and Italy. What may be considered standard by manufacturers in this country may be far wider and longer than the imports that are now available. Many children's-furniture stores have on an average 30 to 33-inch-wide beds because, for most children, this is wide enough and big enough until they are sixteen years old, or older. You can use a single contour bottom sheet and tuck in the slack.

Kinds of Beds   When it is time for a big grown-up bed, have a real grown-up bed, one that will last for as long as your child wants to use it. Buy a good bed which can ultimately be used in the guest room.

Swiss Lattoflex beds have firm flexible wood slats that spring, and good mattresses. They come in a variety of sizes and designs, including a trundle bed which gives you an extra bed without taking up any extra floor space.

I have only one strong recommendation to make regarding your child's bed: Buy a new mattress. If you have an old bed, have a bedding man come and check the box spring and mattress. Your child's back has a long life ahead of it. Doctors advise a firm mattress which could be made of hair or polyurethane foam or rubber. Many children sleep on a low platform made of plywood with a four-inch foam mattress. It is not necessary to have a box spring; in fact, if you have a box spring, check every year or so to see if it's still in one piece. Children are awfully tempted to use a bed with springs as a trampoline which is fun but doesn't help the springs! Whatever your budget or space limitations are, you will be doing the right thing by your child if the bed has a firm mattress. Try to purchase a hospital-quality mattress and be sure the mattress covering is flame resistant.

The bed, after all, is a place where your child spends half his childhood. Get an arrangement you are happy with and make the bed special. Add some life to an ordinary headboard by painting it a solid color and adding hand-painted flowers or soldiers or Snoopy or Pooh Bear. Have some fun and paint it another way in a few years.

Bunk Beds   It's a little early for your two-year-old to be climbing up a ladder to the top bunk; he probably won't be ready to sleep on a top bunk until he's about five. However, you might want to purchase bunk beds now and use only the bottom bunk until the time is right for climbing.

Even before the top bunk is used for sleeping, bunk beds can be fun because the bottom bunk has a "roof" over it, making a cozy lower space. And later, the top bunk is close to the ceiling and therefore cozy for the child who sleeps on top. An extra bunk provides a spare bed for a friend or future sibling.

Deciding which bunk beds to buy isn't easy because there are many good ones to choose from. You might even buy triple bunk beds!

If you are considering bunk beds, be sure to get two single beds (or three) that can be used separately, as well as on top of one another. This is a key point because you never know when you'll want to separate your children into two rooms during an illness, or want to move one bed for an elderly family member who comes to visit. Later, when your children are older and/or no longer thrilled about being in the top bunk (or when you want to separate them), you can use the bunks as useful single beds anywhere. Children enjoy using their child's furniture later on in their adult life. These beds might be in a guest room or even used for your child's own children one day.

If you have single beds used as a bunk bed setup, you will be grateful for this separate-bed flexibility. Two adults can lift the top bed off. Moving is easier with a less cumbersome unit, too, so try and remove the top bed from the bottom bed right in the store where you buy it. If you can't move it there, you won't be able to do it any easier at home! Many bunk bed units can be purchased unassembled. They aren't that difficult to asemble, and it does save you money, especially in trucking bills. And when you move (or when units are being stored), they won't take up as much space. Be sure you understand the instructions before you make your purchase, and when the beds are delivered, count the parts you need to put them together, to be sure no parts are missing. My dentist bought a crib and had to make an impression of one of the missing pieces in order to create one so he could hold the crib together; not all of us are so clever with our hands!

Most bunk bed models that are designed to stack on top of each other have a removable guard rail. This rail is a great safety feature when your two-year-old first adjusts to a regular bed; and certainly it is necessary for the child in the upper bunk. Eventually, when you want to use the beds separately, placed parallel against a wall for sitting as well as sleeping, you can unscrew the front rail.

The Muurame bunk beds designed by Pirkko Stenros, a Finnish architect (purchased at Scandinavian Designs, Inc., or Design Research), are cleanly designed, solidly built, and allow for maximum flexibility. There is a middle piece which separates the two beds, allowing adequate height between the two beds and creating a ladder. You can buy a bookcase that hangs on the side of the bed and also doubles as a night table or an extra surface for the one up top. You can buy drawers on rollers which slide easily underneath the bottom bunk. Buy one long drawer and you have a bed for a baby, a trundle bed, a box, or a storage drawer. Or, buy two square drawers to fit together under the bed unit. Make your own seat and add oars and you have a boat! (Much happiness and play can come from a drawer which can later be used for storage.)

You will not want to use the top bunk for sleeping until your child is a few years older, but soon you could have it used as a play area, or as a roof over the lower bed, as mentioned earlier.

Put a patterned sheet on the bottom of the upper mattress to cover the gray, drab ticking. I also should point out that a disadvantage of bunk beds is they are less flop onable, and a child may bump his head if he's not careful.

I have a personal reason for recommending that you wait until a child is about five before letting him sleep in the top bunk. My four-and-a-half-year-old was sleeping on a top bunk and had to go to the bathroom in the middle of the night. She climbed down the ladder and, because of the dim light, panicked on the ladder halfway down. Tears and fear of falling made this a bad experience. Possibly you can begin slowly by letting your child use the upper bunk for playing and reading so that by the time your child uses it for sleeping it will seem like home.

Other "Bunk Bed" Alternatives Childcraft makes a corner bunk bed unit (in their Paidi collection) with one bed (the upper) along one wall and the lower bed on the adjacent wall. Many units which are set up this way have a small desk area under the upper bunk. The child on the bottom has a roof over the desk space.

Some parents with active children are afraid a child will fall out of the upper bunk. I wouldn't suggest allowing a child to use the upper bunk if the child feels insecure up that high; you can judge when it's time. For extra precaution, place a tumbling mat in front of the bed. You can make your own out of cellular plastic or buy one already covered in washable wear-resistant material.

I know a mother who put a piece of plywood on top of her third-tier bed frame instead of a mattress. (The room had 14-foot ceilings.) She turned the top tier into a horticulture center for her two sons. They hooked on a plant-grow light and grew all sorts of interesting fauna. Someday her three-month-old baby, also a boy, may sleep on that bed frame.

The fact is, children love to climb. Some children are more sensitive to this need than others, but all children love to climb. Erik H. Erikson said, "To climb adds unused dimensions to the awareness of our body. Play here gives a sense of divine leeway, of excess space." I'm sure that shortage of space was the prime reason for the creation of the double-decker bunk bed, and children seem to love them. They save space and add height in a child's place.

Architects, designers, and parents have created a variety of multilevel environments for children which have looked like the inside of a boat; a fire engine; a space ship; loft beds; battleships; trilevel sleep nooks, with slides for down and ladders for up. Pickup trucks provide slides and toy chests and cubbyholes for storage. Some upper beds have slides going down to bouncy platforms below, with swings and jungle gym above. Some rooms have a basketball court and bridges connecting one multipurpose play-sleep-work area with another, all on different levels. Children's rooms today, just like today's children, have come a long way. Creating a multilevel labyrinth of space offers an exciting challenge to even a young child. A child will grow into this kind of arrangement quite naturally and, because of the variety of dimensions and challenges, will equally enjoy using the space for sleep and play.

Canopy Beds If you have a daughter, chances are you might at some point be tempted to indulge in a canopy bed for her. If this notion is in your mind, you don't necessarily have to buy a canopy bed; you might add a canopy to your existing bed. One easy way to create a canopy is to use the upper bunk of a bunk bed as a canopy; put some rods inside and gather a curtain on three sides. The front might have a pair of curtains tied back. Be sure to install a rod along the head and the foot of the bed, right under the wires that hold the upper mattress in place; then stretch a piece of material from one rod to the other, to form a curtain under the mattress above and to hide the wires—the inside of the top is important. When your daughter is inside her bed, it will be like being inside a pretty box.

If you are buying a new bed, inquire how a canopy could be added at a later date. I saw a particularly attractive canopy bed which had an iron canopy, painted white and covered in cotton eyelet. This was made to be added to an ordinary wood frame.

Bedcoverings I haven't discussed bedcovers at length because they are the relatively easy part. Here, flexibility and easy care are the most important. Don't drape your child's bed in an expensive quilted print and go to the expense of custom labor to make a fitted spread, and then have to worry about spills. Why make the bed off limits for fun? Household accidents happen in all relaxed households where normal children are growing up. Plan on it. We were brought up in an era where beds were always inspection ready, and we were not allowed to be on our beds except when we were sick or when it was time to go to sleep. Now, with space limitations and a new understanding about a child having his own private place, his bed is his bed and he will be on it a whole lot more than you might think.

A heavy bedspread is not necessary. A thinner cover, one your child can eventually manage without help from an adult, is frequently the best solution. Look for snuggly soft blankets that feel good to the touch, in warm colors or a plaid you like; blankets should be machine washable and in colors that won't show the dirt. An inexpensive quilt is an excellent solution. Your child's bed is no place to use an old army blanket. A child's blanket should be a soft colorful one, and then you won't have to hide it under a spread.

Or, take two and a half yards of wide cotton material and hem the two cut ends. The selvage sides don't really need any hem because they won't ravel. Buy several remnants of fabric so you can make the bed in a variety of different colors and patterns, changing them as easily as you would the sheets underneath. Just as you select a different tablecloth for a dinner party, a choice of inexpensive bedcovers can offer the excitement of change. These covers can be machine washed and ironed, folded up and stored right in the linen closet when not in use on the bed. The variety is pleasant and if there is an accident, it really isn't hard to clean up—and you'll have several different bedcovers handy as substitutes. These tuck right in and look neat and trim.

If you have a box spring that is exposed and you need to cover it with a flounce, select a color which will go with just about anything you put on top of the bed. If your child is particularly accident prone, maybe you'd consider a vinyl flounce cover. One wipe and it's clean. And, if your experience is that there are constant spills in bed, you can have your material coated with clear plastic; this lets the design show and yet the fabric can be cleaned simply by wiping it with a sponge.

Sheets   One of the nicest things that has happened is the special designs for children, and manufacturers tell me that their biggest volume is in their juvenile lines. Parents now can give their child personal identity just by buying a set of sheets. You can have Peanuts, Mickey Mouse, Raggedy Ann, "bears in my bed," a botanical zoo. You can have bold stripes or soft lilies of the valley. Taking your child to buy sheets for his first bed can be as exciting as buying him his first pair of new shoes. Many of these sheet companies have quilted, lightweight comforters to match, and they are a snap for a child to throw over a bed. Each year new designs are added and old ones dropped. I know families whose children trade sheets—"I'll take the duck and the swan for your Snoopy." One set of sheets we've had for years is still a favorite —a farmhouse with a pond and trees and flowers. The colors are still fresh and clear. This sheet has long been discontinued, so when you do find one you like, buy it right away because next fall might be too late. Familiar sheets provide a touch of home when they get shipped off to camp. Sheets in whimsical and lively designs are the same price as ordinary sheets and require no ironing.

Quilts and Things Made by Hand   If you have an old quilt you've acquired through the years, you might use it as a colorful wall hanging for a child's room. Small ones can be folded at the foot of a bed as a touch of color and design and pulled up when needed. Cotton quilts machine wash beautifully.

Bed Things   Children love their beds, and love to fill them with dolls and stuffed animals and favorite blankets. By putting a quilt or extra blanket at the foot of the bed, you can further enclose the space. Later, when the child grows and can use the length of the bed for growing legs, you can shed a few layers of stuffed animals, dolls, bolsters, and pillows. During the earlier years, it feels good to touch these friends and familiar things. Some people feel a child should not be allowed to sleep with dolls or favorite Snoopy or teddy bear. I disagree. A safe doll or stuffed animal can act as security and comfort to a child who is otherwise alone while sleeping. Regular pillows are not good for posture, so it's better for young children to sleep with small baby pillows. Some children develop allergies and if your child does, your doctor will advise you what is best for your child's particular needs. If your child is free of special problems, you have to make your own rules about the bed companions—safety first.

Chest of Drawers   Besides the crib or bed, furniture requirements at this stage are simple; space is your real need. A chest of drawers with drawers that are operative by a small child is a blessing for both parents and child. Drawers should slide effortlessly and be in sympathetic scale to a child's small frame.

Study the way the joints on the drawers are put together; be sure they are dovetailed and glued, not nailed. Make sure the bottom of the drawer can withstand weight. Children play with their furniture, so it has to be sturdy. Be certain your child can reach both knobs on a drawer without straining. Many designs don't require knobs at all, but rather there is an indentation on the face of each drawer for fingers to pull. Be sure the drawers have stops if you have any high drawers; a sharp drawer edge can be dangerous.

A child is an insatiable explorer of new levels. Encourage with furniture; don't discourage. Uplift your child's motives with designs he or she can manage. Pay more for functional designs. Examine each piece to assure yourself that you are getting a solid piece of furniture.

Furniture Height   If the chest of drawers is low (as low as 21 to 23 inches), the top surface can act as a work area for your child. And, also, you don't waste drawer space because the top drawers are too high for your child to see inside. The average table height is 20 inches high for small people.

Furniture Systems   You might try to find chests of drawers in various widths which can be used as a group, with one common top. This can create a flexible, growing arrangement, and give a clean cohesive appearance to this busy activity room.

When you select any piece of furniture to use for storage, try to find one with the appropriate design and scale you won't get tired of, as storage needs expand. If you buy a chest 21 inches wide, with three drawers, in six years you might want to buy another, to make a pair; and then you could put a 44-inch top over them, creating a furniture complex that can be used as a desk. If you have more than one child's room to think of, consider compatible designs that might one day be combined. You never know what future circumstances will make it necessary for your children to share a room. Always remember, pairs can be separated, but separates don't always pair well. Design is more important than color. (Color is flexible and can be changed or combined.) Buy open-stock furniture whenever you can. Think of furniture as a system.

Color of Furniture I personally feel that dark brown wood furniture looks heavy when it is used in a room for small children. If a room is small, it appears more so when the massive appearance of dark wood pieces is added. Find simple, inexpensive light woods; if the piece is unfinished, seal it with a clear, protective shellac, which can give the room an uplift.

Painted furniture is light and offers more decorative possibilities. Paint does chip, however, so if you don't want to repaint or touch up from time to time, avoid painted furniture. There are new stains you can get in intense, lively colors which are every bit as practical as a brown stain. Don't choose a bizarre, trendy color; it might become tiresome in a few months.

Vinyl, Metal, and Plastic Furniture Vinyl, metal, and plastic furniture is excellent for a child's room; it can be wiped clean with any household cleaner, and it is light enough for a child to move about. Avoid plastic Parson's tables at this age because the edges are too sharp. I recommend that if you choose furniture made of one of these materials, you stay with white whenever possible. Plastics can't be painted over successfully. White will fit in with anything else you have in the room. Also you might eventually tire of bold colors, and they become even more burdensome when you can't paint over them.

Metal furniture can be painted, but it should be sprayed, not painted with a brush.

A white laminated top surface is the most practical. The sides of furniture don't get quite the same abuse as the tops, so the legs and apron (the piece of material under the top surface which often holds drawers) can be of wood if that fits your plans best. If you have a good piece of furniture you don't want ruined, have a thin laminated top made for use during these vigorous early years—one you can remove later.

Furniture Placement Furniture placement is important for practicality, and also it can be used to create a feeling of intimacy. As a general rule, think of keeping your large furniture pieces against the wall to allow as much free floor space as possible. However, it might seem like a huge gymnasium to your child, without barriers in center field. A jungle gym, a slide, a sandbox, or seesaw, placed to the side of the room, might easily be rolled or moved to the center when it's in use. Anything you put in the center of the room should be easily movable for times when more space is called for. Lightweight tables and child chairs lend themselves to festive room changes, with only slight

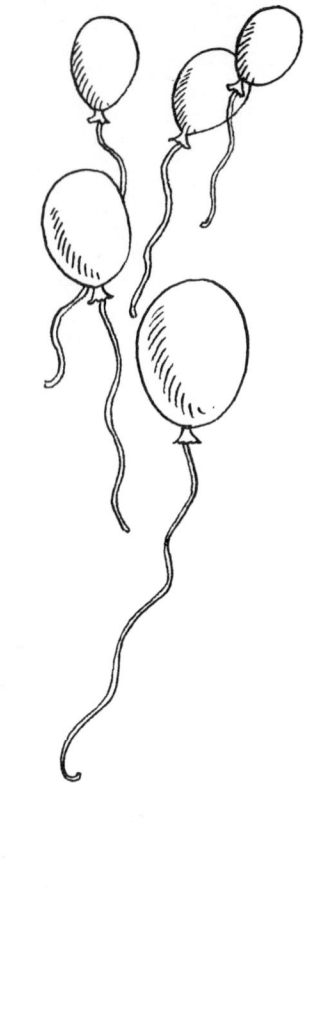

repositioning. Think in terms of creating clearly designed interest areas.

The Floor Is a Table At this age, the floor is a good table. Birthday parties are easily created right on the floor, with balloons, a paper party tablecloth (clear plastic underneath to catch the spills), paper cups, and the joy of chocolate drips and ice cream swirls. A large blanket can be spread over the floor with a quarter-inch rubber pad underneath, to create a warmer play area when the toddler is not toddling around the room.

STORAGE

The Closet You can build adjustable shelves inside a closet simply by using inexpensive metal strips (called "standards") which have holes in them for the brackets that hold the shelves. If you decide to use a closet for storing your child's clothes, toys, and materials, be sure you remember how low the shelves must be for the child's reach, not yours. When your child stands, the ideal height for a shelf is waist-high. When he or she grows a few inches, simply raise the shelf.

Closed storage space is best for most areas, to maintain an uncluttered appearance.

Closet Door—Some Alternatives Remember to be certain the closet door is easy to open and the handle is low enough for a small child to reach. If not, possibly you can remove the door for a year or so (if it is too heavy and cumbersome for a small child to manage). You might replace it with lighter half doors made of wooden slats. Or, an easier solution might be to loop a brightly colored printed bed sheet (which you can have flame-proofed) through a rod. (There is a heading on all sheets for this purpose.) Or, get a thin piece of plywood, paint it a lively color, add a yellow circle or a green diagonal stripe, and install it on a hinge. Or, cut it in two, making a Dutch door. Children will love this because it is "their height," it is easy to manage, and they can use it later to play "candy store," or post office and for puppet shows, and other games. Many apartment buildings have extra doors in the basement so if you move, or when your child is older, you can put a solid door back on the hinges.

FUN HOUSE

The whole idea in planning for this age and the next is to make the entire space a "fun house." Your child is young and small, and this place is his. Why have it be a room with a few token young ideas? Or, just a place to sleep. Toy stores sell expensive dollhouses and big environmental structures for children's rooms, but few of us can afford them; and, also, why go to the expense of buying an additive when you have the entire space to develop and can have the pleasure of creating better, more imaginative things for this space right at home? There is no need for a playroom when your child's bedroom can be the playroom. Remember, there is no need for one extra piece of furniture or one extra thing that isn't appreciated and happily used by your child.

A PLAYPEN

A crib is designed not only for a child's safety, but also for the parents' convenience, and it is one exception I think is a good one. A playpen, however, seems to me strictly a convenience for the parents and something to be used rarely. A playpen doesn't provide enough variation of play or space for crawling and moving around, to be used regularly. Instead, think of the whole room as a playpen. Use a gate at the door or the Dutch door idea so you can see your child at play. The entire room, whatever the dimension, can be thought of as the play area. And only use the playpen on occasion.

DOLLHOUSE

Instead of buying a dollhouse, use a big brown carton and decorate it. A bookcase shelf also makes a good dollhouse. Or, have your child help you create a house. In this child's place you and your child actively work and play and build.

Beyond the Basics

Now that we've discussed the basic elements for a child's place during the eight-months-to-three-year period, here are some ad-

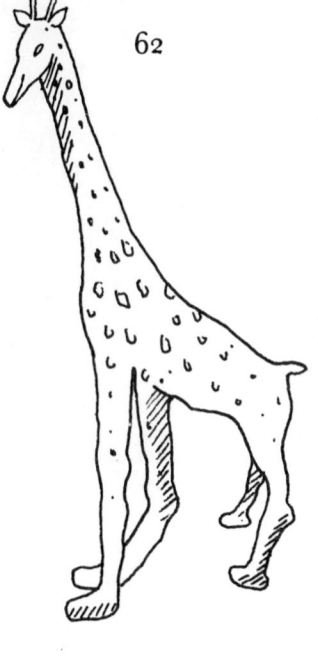

ditional ideas for frivolous things you might add, according to your sense of what your developing child might like.

1. *Make a platform.* A 4-by-8-foot plywood platform for romping and creative activities. Join four 8-foot-by-12-inch panels together. Cut the four corners round; sand and paint the top a solid-color deck enamel and the bottom in a nondirectional pattern of colors and shapes. This platform can be rigged up on a dolly to drop down from the ceiling on ropes so that it can be ready in an instant or out of the way safely, when not in use. Or, it can remain as a stationary unit, on the floor, until the child is older, and raising or lowering the platform from the ceiling will seem more feasible. It creates an ideal surface for group finger-painting or serious block building. Some people make these platforms with a two-inch lip all around, to provide a traylike surface for paints and projects. This platform can be used for future plays, puppet shows, birthday parties, and slumber parties. It saves space, time, and money.

2. *Make a giant giraffe of felt.* Have some fun creating a gooney giraffe so your child can measure his own exciting growth. Be sure the giraffe has a long neck so that a cloth tape measure can be sewn from its leg to the top of its head. Attach it to the wall with two-sided carpet tape. Children are intrigued by their own growth, and you and your child can have fun measuring his progress.

3. *Colorful cushions.* Buy big sheets of polyfoam and cut them into a variety of shapes, approximately 16 inches to 18 inches—a few circles, a few triangles, some squares, some rectangles, a hexagonal, an octagonal, and a few odd shapes. Buy some inexpensive stretch material in different colors and wrap these polyfoam shapes, keeping sewing to a minimum; use Velcro to close the opening so you can easily remove the covers to wash them. Velcro is available in colors as well as in white, and it sticks together easily. These cushions will be used to create special places, to snuggle with, sit on, and toss around in play.

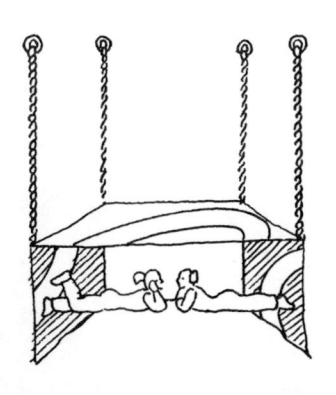

4. *Hang panels of colorful fabric looped from the ceiling.* To lower the ceiling and create a bright tentlike feeling, take a four- or five-yard piece of brightly printed cotton material and insert small plastic rings on the two selvages (both sides of the width) one yard apart. On the ceiling area where you want the fabric (over the bed or in a play corner), insert screw eyes the width of the material, to receive the rings of the panels of fabric; put the

face side of the fabric toward the floor. In order to get the fullness in the loops, have the ceiling hooks two feet apart. (Vary the distances for an irregular effect.) If your ceiling is very high, have the rings on your fabric farther apart (48 inches) and your ceiling screw eyes closer together, say, 32 inches to lower the panels. Merrimekko is the ideal fabric for this use and can be purchased at Design Research; the designs and colors are whimsical and lively and will never be outgrown. When the child is older they can be reused as wall panels, bedspreads, or curtains. For now, this lowered ceiling height gives a sense of enclosure, adds excitement and color.

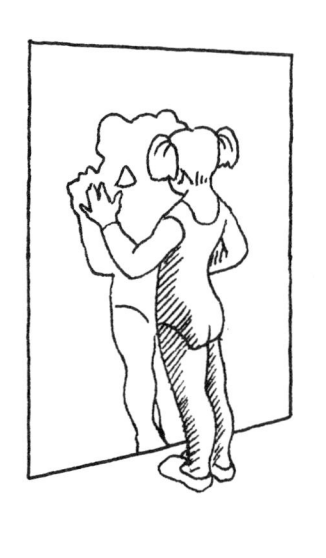

You could change these panels from time to time for variety.

5. *Provide secondary spaces—space within space.* Children love to be enclosed. Hang from strong hook eyes screwed into the ceiling a simple A-frame "roof," made from plywood and canvas, in a bright color; support this tent from the roof by a chain. The chain will make the "tent" move. Put this in the corner of a small room or in the center of a large room. Children this age don't like too big an unbroken space. For added fantasy, hang down triangular flaps which can be unfurled to the floor. They switch around when touched by the child and are excellent for peek-a-boo. This place becomes personal and warm and cozy. Big play pillows on the floor work beautifully to complete this fun house.

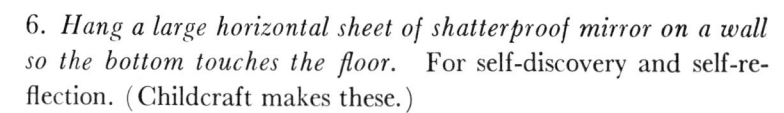

6. *Hang a large horizontal sheet of shatterproof mirror on a wall so the bottom touches the floor.* For self-discovery and self-reflection. (Childcraft makes these.)

7. *Make a boat.* Remove hinges and top, then paint the bottom portion of a huge steamer trunk; line with pads and pillows and make it into a wonderful boat.

8. *Create a multilevel environment* on the floor by covering plywood shapes and planes in inexpensive carpeting that has been glued on. As stated earlier, climbing adds dimensions of awareness to the child. Each section has its own special message to the child, and he or she will associate certain toys and games and activities with each area. (A jungle gym with a practical purpose.)

Make this with two solid panels, 24 inches high, supporting an irregular-shaped top. On the top, build plywood partitions like a dimensional jigsaw puzzle. Later, kids use this table for a dollhouse, a farm or display area for treasures.

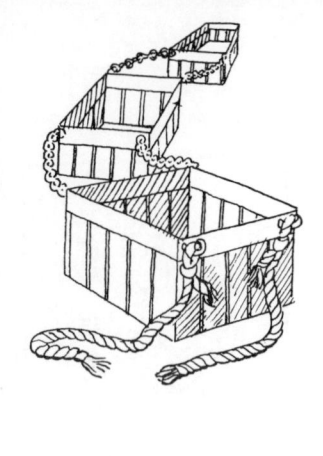

9. *Make a train* out of orange crates. Glue felt to the bottom so the child can slide the train around. Attach the "cars" with chain bought from the hardware store and loop a jump rope through the "engine" car for the child to use as a pull. This way two children can pull together. These cars can be useful as blocks and for toy storage, after play. You can substitute colored toy bins for the orange crates if you prefer.

10. *Make some stairs.* Construct a series of wood steps with a railing, paint them, and install a runner or carpeting. Attach these steps to a wall with the top step about 30 inches high, wide enough to allow space for play. Children love to climb stairs. You might even be able to buy a portion of a staircase from a demolition site or local wrecking company.

11. *Make a multisurface table* of inexpensive pine lumber and bolt it to the floor with angle irons so the toddler can climb up by himself. Instead of a flat table, have the surface look like a block construction. These different surface shapes and sizes create walls for the child's imaginative play. Paint these multilevel compartments in wildly bright and gentle pastel colors for contrast.

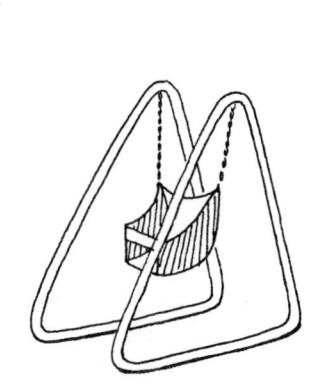

12. *Make or buy a playhouse.* There are many playhouses commercially available, or you might make one yourself. Have a lumberyard cut you four plywood panels each 4 feet by 4 feet. Paint each panel, or "wall" a different color inside and out. Attach the walls together with removable pin hinges. Cut out curves and holes and windows and a door. On the floor, add a foam mat covered with a blanket or soft fabric remnant, toss in some pillows, and let your children romp and explore. This can be knocked down easily and stored flat under a bed.

13. *Buy an indoor-gym house* with a blue slide, a small red ladder, and a round circle for play inside. Inexpensive for its value, safe, durable, and an aid to sound physical development. (Childcraft)

14. *Buy a toddler's gym* with a four-foot climbing tower, separate steps, oak ladder, and a four-foot slide. This is good for children up to five years of age. (Child Life Play Specialties, Inc.)

15. *Add an inexpensive deluxe baby swing* with high sides, secure seat, front safety strap, and braided ropes. Comes complete. (Child Life Play Specialties, Inc.)

16. *Add a small rocking chair.*
    In the next chapter we will discuss room changes, where your child becomes the originator rather than the participator.

Chapter 4

GROWING UP
(ages three to eight)

I shall like to recapture that freshness of vision
which is characteristic of extreme youth, when
all the world is new to it.

HENRI MATISSE

More than most nations we have defined children as future producers and have valued or devalued them accord-
ingly. The qualities that we have tried to implant in them
have been the traits thought necessary for power and
status in our economic system. The question we confront
today is whether it is possible for our society to begin to
define children in some other way—a way that empha-
sizes the fulfillment of their potential as unique individuals with a diversity of talents.

KENNETH KENISTON,
Professor of Psychology at Yale
Yale Alumni Magazine, April 1974.

I would rather see a wonderful child than the Grand Canyon.

The Art Spirit
ROBERT HENRI

After the crib stage, a child is old enough to be encouraged to play an active role in the design of his or her room. If you provide the basics and the background, your child can then be free to create different schemes, based on what he or she is like, against the backdrop of the basic design elements you have provided. By the age of three most children are ready.

Also, this is the period when a child's own place, for his own activities, becomes increasingly important. He needs you near, but he also needs lots of space to play, to experiment for hours.

This is also, in many ways, the period when the child is most focused on play at home, when he will spend the most concentrated hours of play at home. In the next period, more time will be spent at school, camp, or at the homes of friends. But now, his own place at home is the real center of activity.

THE KEY: "BALANCED" DEVELOPMENT

Dr. White points out in his book mentioned earlier, *The First Three Years of Life,* the importance of suitable playthings and materials. During this period, also, growth and challenging experiences can be especially encouraged through playthings, environment, and by involving children in co-operative activity. This stage of soaring imagination, curiosity about others, can be an invaluable learning time, a time when, with a parent's help, the child can take a more active role in shaping his or her own child's place.

CREATIVITY

In a dollhouse-design course I once gave, I learned again how impossible it is to take anything for granted when it comes to children. Each student in this course for six-to-eight-year-olds was given an eighteen-inch-square brown box. The students were allowed to do anything they wanted with their boxes. We discussed the concept of creating an environment inside the box, of the box being used to house the colors, forms, designs, and feelings most enjoyable to the student. "Am I allowed to make mine a garden?" "Does mine have to be my own bedroom?"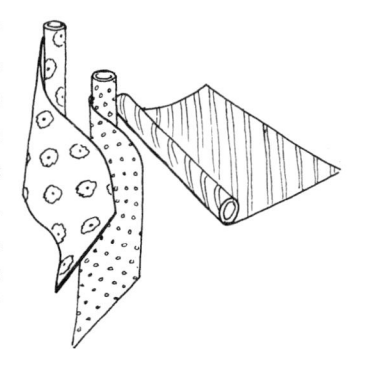

"Am I allowed to divide it into more than one room?" "Am I supposed to decorate the outside?" "May I change the shape of my box?" Every question was handled with individual attention because these questions were all clues. The answer usually was, yes, you may do anything you wish.

Each student was also given basic materials—wallpaper, rugs, Magic Markers, fabric swatches, scissors, glue, two-sided tape, and lots of small, seemingly useless, household items.

Empty spools of thread were created into end tables. Wooden coffee stirrers were used to make posts on a canopy bed. Rock brown sugar was the soil for a horticulturalist who made a formal Italian garden. The top of a can of shaving cream was a lamp shade. A lace doily was colored and decorated to be used as a hook rug on a kitchen floor. Paper cups were cut in such a way that they became modern "plastic barrel-back chairs." Small blocks of wood were painted to become beds, sofas, end tables, and headboards. Bigger pieces of wood were used for making lofts and second stories. This was the way it began. We asked the students to bring in treasures from home—anything at all was all right as long as the child felt it could be adapted in some way to the project. We suggested they cut out pictures from magazines of things they liked, or gather things they liked. Leaves, shells, noodles were brought into class. One girl was creating such a sophisticated structure with cantilevered terraces and spiral staircases (made from folding and piecing together corrugated paper) that I inquired what her parents did. "They're both architects." The imagination and creative input was inspirational. I realized that these children didn't want it to end with an eighteen-inch cardboard box, they wanted to create their own rooms. This is especially true as a child gets older.

HOW TO HELP YOUR CHILD SET UP HIS ROOM

How do you begin to set up this room? Ask your child, "What can we do to make your room work better for you?" Asking your child how he wants his room arrangement is no different from asking him, for example, what he wants from Santa for Christmas, or for his birthday; and if he wants things that are too expensive, say so, and help him work out substitutes. Or, if he wants a bunk bed and the one he admires is too expensive, you might make your own. Or suggest another type of bed. If TV in the room is against your better judgment, explain why.

Your child can express his own style and taste within the restrictions of your ability to go along with them. The main thing is that he or she should feel this room is really his place, a place that is set up by, and for, his activities.

THE ORGANIZER

"Want to see my room?" The instinct to nest is strong in man and beast, and it doesn't take long before your child has it. This is the time to let your child help design her own environment. Let the child be the organizer rather than merely the participant. Your child's opinions and personal feelings are the beginnings of a strong need to escape from the nest and create his own place. Guide the child to fulfill whatever is strongest and deepest in his unique personality. This urge is instinctive. Encourage individual feelings by providing a room that reflects your child's own thought.

A PERSONAL ENVIRONMENT

When a child has a hand in building a personal environment, pride is automatic. Curiosity and imagination are encouraged by bringing out the child's own sense of self and freedom. If the room is just the way he wants it, what better place is there under the sun? Self-expression will be developed more quickly and naturally if encouraged in these beginning years.

Listen to the clues from your child. By treating your child's suggestions seriously, you help a child develop much-needed self-confidence—a feeling of importance. Ownership is a strong need, too. It is important for a child to have things to love and care for, many of which will be contained in his private place.

The child's room may become a baby sitter; your son or daughter will want to putter around in it by the hour.

As each child is different, so too there need not be much that is stereotyped about a child's room. No two rooms need look alike, even though they will be made up of similar elements. The plainer and simpler the elements, the more unstructured items free from detail, the more room there is for the child to be creative and to grow.

KEEP THE BASIC ROOM SIMPLE

So keep the basic room simple. Have it bare and uncluttered, with clean bright walls, easy-care floor, lots of storage places, a regular "big" bed. If there's extra space, include an extra bookcase; it will be filled up in time. Before it is used for books, it might be a dollhouse or a display area or a play area for miniature cars and trucks or animals. Provide shelves for storing games, puzzles, records, supplies, and treasures. Keep colorful empty plastic or rubber tote boxes in a stack for the child's own future use. Try to create a "cozy corner" for quiet times, in the midst of a room set up for action. You don't need to decorate for your child, or impose your floor plan on him. By providing the simple basics, you can give your child a solid foundation on which to build, to personalize her own place, and to develop a greater sense of her own identity and interests in the process.

Encourage in your child freedom of choice, within reasonable bounds. Ask your child if she wants a red desk chair or a yellow one. Does he have a preference for sleeping at the head or the foot of the bed? Does he want his bed in a corner or in the center of things? High or low? Where should his bed be placed? Ask. Little things may mean more to the child than we realize, and you can guide him in making his choices.

One mother painted her daughter's room white and striped all the moldings pink. It was feminine and charming and perfect for Blair. The adjoining room was the home of Blair's older brother, William. The idea spread: "Wouldn't it be a good idea to paint William's room white and stripe his moldings blue?" When the children were away on a short vacation, the room was painted. It looked fine, but it had been done without the consent, or support, of nine-year-old William, who hated the blue and wished his room were back the old way. The poor mother was furious that her ungrateful child did not appreciate her hard work; this needn't have happened if William had been consulted.

COLOR

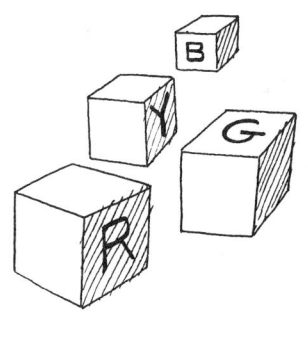

During this entire age group, color will continue to grow in importance for your child. Color remains one of the great learning tools. By the age of three, children are taught reading readiness through color recognition. Colors are symbols and tools, and children recognize colors and personally identify with them. New mathematics is taught to four-year-olds with Cuisenaire colored rods—colored wooden rectangular rods which use color substitutes for value, so mathematical concepts can be more easily developed. In our knowledge-oriented society, we are told, everyone will be relying increasingly on mathematics. Most children find these colorful blocks (or rods) more fun and more tactically stimulating than $2+2=4$. Red is smaller than yellow, light green is smaller than purple, dark green is bigger than yellow. Your child will grow in knowledge and pleasure through his identification and association with color throughout this important early school period.

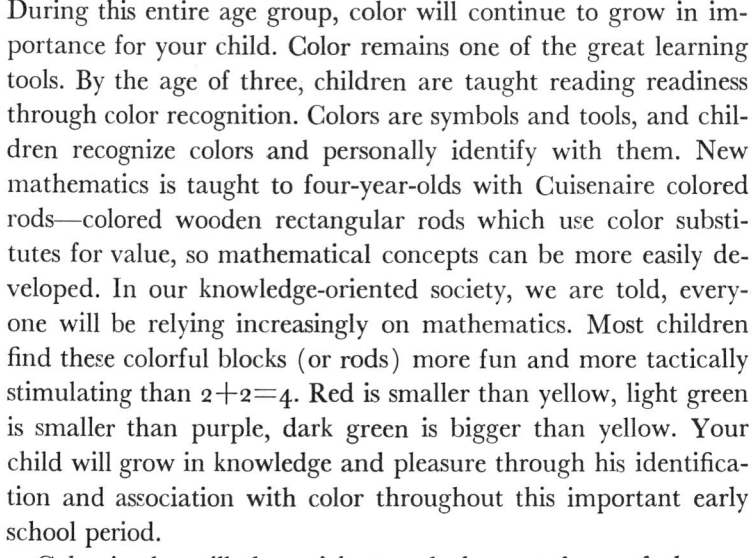

Color is also still the quickest and cheapest form of change. Give your child strong white paper and some good paint supplies. At this age the child loves big white pads of paper and the best water-color pencils, felt-tipped markers, and multiple-medium crayons. Little artists need quality supplies just as much as older artists. Indulge in a few tubes of intensely colored acrylic paint; buy a large tube of white and watch the magic appear.

For most of this age period, color is the chief means of expression. Encourage this in the child's place. Try and get hold of a roll of some no-seam paper, the kind used in photographic studios, so the child's creativity can unroll freely, as the urge hits.

TASTE

If you allow your child freedom of expression in his own room, most children will be strongly imitative of what they have absorbed from their parents as well as what they have picked up from other influences. Taste stems from this exposure and children seem to get it through osmosis; and, at this age, "good taste" can be encouraged to develop. The absorption that takes place is like a sponge sopping up milk. By being exposed to colors, ideas, and customs, your child may assimilate your ideas,

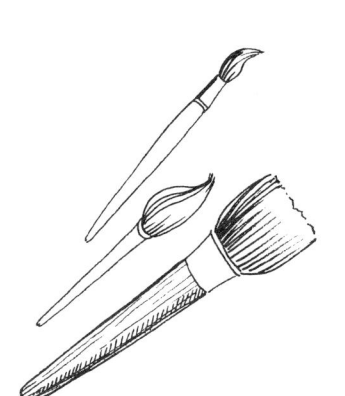

what you believe to be "the way." If you are secure and happy in what you do, it is natural for your child to want to copy you. "If Mommy likes it, it must be good." It is usually when parents overreact, and force issues, that children are turned off and become contrary. Basically, children seek a parent's approval, or praise. Unconsciously, little girls like to imitate their mothers. If Mother is a feminine creature, Lara wants to dress up in high heels and lipstick. In spite of exceptions, it's obvious that parents do influence their children in big and small ways, when they want to and even when they're tryng not to. Help your child develop design taste by guiding him as he tries things in his own place.

Don't be surprised or discouraged if your child doesn't pick up every one of your good habits right away; or if your ideas about texture and color schemes aren't incorporated immediately into his room. It took you years to get where you are in your thinking; let your child take time too. Let him go his own way as much as possible, for as long as he needs to, and respect his feelings as long as they are real and honest.

One mother came to me in horror when she used my theory on her six-year-old by asking the child: "What colors would you like in your room?" "Black and white!" To this day (six years later), Allison has one of the most attractive, chic bedrooms I've ever seen. Spanking white walls, white swiss tambour-embroidered curtains, a shining mirror, black-and-white checkerboard floor, a black canopy bed with a beautiful multicolored patchwork quilt her mother made. Black and white doesn't mean you can't add other colors. Allison's mother proved willing to give her daughter's idea a try, and together they were able to embark on one of the most fun-filled design adventures of their lives. When your children see you actively involved in the execution of their ideas, the impression is indelible. The love bond is permanent; the pleasure shared is special.

PLENTY OF STORAGE PLACES

Every person needs storage, and bins such as the ones mentioned earlier in the chapter are good for toys. The heavy-duty plastic stackable toy bins have holes on two sides to use as handgrips.

Take your son or daughter to the hardware or department store and let the child pick a color. Your child may prefer three different colors which will set the color tone for his room. If there is more than one kind to choose from and they are comparable in price, ask. Children can be particular about what food they like, what clothes to wear, how dolls are dressed; most children will have a preference about design elements, too, if you ask. Should you ask, follow the advice you get as much as you can.

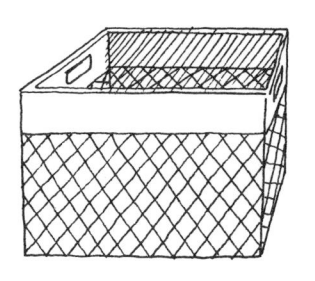

A variety of multistorage units designed for children's use is commercially available. The most important feature of a good storage unit is that there be many different separate compartments which allow for versatility of use. You can't have one big shelf and say, "Here, put all your things away." Puzzles should have their own slots, as should games and toys. There should be separate tote bins for materials and small items, to keep them together. Many storage units come with a separate base so they can be easily moved around the room. Large sturdy wooden bins (square or rectangular) on casters can be stored under the bed in otherwise wasted space and are available where children's furniture is sold. These can double as trains and cars at playtime; the only drawback is that they do not have separate compartments. Rubber bins (available at houseware stores) can be used to make good separations inside these wooden storage boxes, and they can be set aside when the box is needed for active play.

Nesting Boxes   Community Playthings also sells nesting wooden boxes that slide under the bed; they have tops and are good for storing blocks and other small toys. These boxes also make wonderful doll's beds, or a house for stuffed animals, and they can be useful for general storage for a lifetime.

Storage Cupboard   Have a cupboard with a door on a swing hinge, with a hole for a small hand to pull the door open. Have heavy-duty hooks for smocks and sweaters. You can buy brightly colored plastic "sky" hooks which hold up to thirty pounds; all you do is stick them to a wall surface. If you have more than one child; select a color for each child so the colored hooks are personal. Continue to use the closet in inventive ways for storage "out of sight." By this age, the child should find a regular closet door easy to handle.

ONE CHILD'S PLACE

One of the most exciting children's room arrangements I've ever seen was organized and set up by a four-year-old, and I'm going to tell about it in some detail because it shows how a child's fresh perspective can lead to an effective design arrangement, and also in case some of Sara's ideas might work for you. Sara's visual perception and spacial relations were so advanced in sensitivity for her age that I feel sure she will become an architect or an engineer someday. Before she was five she was well on her way.

Sara's parents knew they would be moving in a few years, so they didn't want to invest in built-in furniture, and they also thought a cluttered child's room was undesirable. So they bought a generous quantity of movable storage units—narrow and wide chests of drawers and hinged cabinet units in rectangular shapes. These ample storage units were of a size suitable for adult use, so they could be used until Sara left home.

Sara's first idea was to create a low fortress out of the storage units in the room; she placed the objects playfully in the center of her space, and then filled them with her puzzles, dolls, and toys, as well as clothes. Eventually the space may be used for bigger things and for more clothes.

There's no such thing as "too many drawers." Sara's sturdy wooden furniture (called "Muurame") was designed by Pirkko Stenros. Go to a showroom where it is on display, to see the versatility of this well-designed furniture which can be used throughout a person's lifetime. It is made of birch and sprayed with many coats of a lead-free plastic paint which gives it a smooth lacquered look. Sara and her mother decided on all-white units, though there was a choice of red, yellow, blue, or white or any combination of these colors. (For example, you could have red units with white drawers or a white unit and red drawers.)

Because the furniture is low, white, and placed on the floor in the middle of the room, it conveys a light, floating feeling. The furniture is finished on all sides. This freestanding arrangement makes sense because the units can be approached from all four sides, making it twice as useful and providing more fun for a child. Also, the units double as space dividers.

"My bedroom has to make my bed the most important thing in my room." In the very center of Sara's 14-by-19-foot room is her bed: a well-sanded piece of plywood (39 by 78 inches), with rounded edges and painted with white enamel paint. On top of this plywood frame is a twin-size mattress covered with a throw of laminated plastic Marimekko cotton print. The five-inch thick hair mattress was an extra one not in use elsewhere in the house, and by using it on the plywood base, the family saved the expense of purchasing a real bed. Sara feels comfortable being so close to the floor and likes the furniture enclosure on two sides. This bed is a perfect place for sleep or play. Sara sleeps in her Raggedy Ann sleeping bag and is surrounded by her dolls and animals. Even Humpty Dumpty has his legs hanging over the wall.

On one side of her bed is a pair of white two-drawer units. One end of the bed has two similar units, with a space in the middle for a kneehole; on top of this hole is a board to use as a desk. (The kneehole is three feet wide so the desk can grow.) The chests are solid enough to actually invite children to sit on them; some of the wood tops are covered with thin (one inch) foam rubber pads in shiny vinyl. The rest of the tops are used for puzzles, checkers, and display areas.

The furniture doesn't appear very high when Sara is in bed or playing on her elevated platform bed because the 11-inch height of the wood platform and mattress lower the height of the surrounding chests of drawers. The drawers have slides on the sides made of plastic, so the drawers are easy for a child to open. The drawer joints are glued and doweled, making them sturdy for the abuse ahead. Sara has a drawer for art supplies, a drawer for games and puzzles, several toy drawers, a costume drawer, and drawers for her clothes. In one secret bottom drawer there is an entire farm with animals—horses, cows, pigs, and sheep, a barn, and farm workers. In another secret drawer are her infants— "babies" tucked in bed with blankets and booties.

These units can be moved around and eventually may be stacked on top of each other and go up against a wall. But for now, Sara has a play-sleep-work area in her scale and in the spirit of this four-year-old.

The arrangement suited Sara to a tee; the furniture created a room-within-a-room feeling because of its placement in the center, which left all four walls free to be used for murals, paintings, or work at a wall-hung easel and blackboard. These walls were, to Sara, the outer walls of her house. The 19-foot wall had no window, so her mother painted in two windows and painted flowering window boxes in a blaze of chromatic colors. There were hills painted, mountains, and a big orange sun, low on the horizon (as if about to set)—the perfect height for Sara to stand

and draw faces or pictures in the sun with chalk. Any latex paint with a satin finish is suitable for a wall mural like this. Or you can buy blackboard paint; or spray in black or green. The green could be used for the mountains, and your child could chalk in an army of ants or soldiers or a field of buttercups.

ANOTHER EXAMPLE

One mother of four spirited children set up their rooms in simple, plain, practical designs. There is little decoration or ornamentation that isn't childlike. One day when all the children were at school, a friend was snooping around in their rooms. She seemed horrified that there weren't bedspreads and curtains and fluffy rugs on the floor. Noting the walls had obviously just been painted (each one a different color), Mrs. Matthew's friend turned to her and asked, "What do you plan to use for the curtains and for a bedspread?" Shutters were at the windows and colored patterned sheets with solid-color blankets were on the beds, but the rooms did seen unfinished when the children weren't playing in them! That is the way a child's room should appear if it is a workable room. (School classrooms are the same way.)

Here are some ideas about the basic room elements:

WALLS

At this age children can express themselves freely with form and color, so their own art work can take up much of the wall space. Therefore, it's a good idea to keep the walls light in color and fairly plain, as in the earlier periods.

The Desire for Pattern If your little girl is very feminine and you and she want her to have a flowered wallpaper, preselect several papers that create an all-over background effect—flowers, or another pattern that isn't too large in scale or overpowering in color. If the pattern is a floral design, examine the leaves and stems carefully. What you see in the wallpaper book and what your daughter will live with later might not appear the same, once it is hung on four walls. Ask how big the repeat is. If you have any doubts, be on the safe side—buy a roll (or get a substantial sample), Scotch tape it to the wall, and study it. Check it in daylight and at night. This is especially important as wallpapers sometimes look beautiful in a flood of sunlight, but at night parts of the design jump out and appear to move around, in a disturbing way. A soft palette, well defined, is better for a flowered wallpaper or wall vinyl.

Vinyl There are many beautiful flower designs on the market today in vinyl. However, it would be wise to select a paper-backed, washable vinyl wallpaper. (You can't hang another wallpaper over vinyl, however, so if you redecorate you would have to remove the vinyl, which can be a chore. However, you can paint over and, if the walls are in poor condition, paint-on vinyl lasts longer than paint on a poor wall. Another advantage, of course, is that vinyl can be washed.) Whether you select plain or pattern, a vinyl wallcovering for this three-to-eight age group is probably preferable to paper. One word of warning: ball-point pens will permanently stain a vinyl wallcovering.

Bulletin Board If you and your child decide on a patterned wallcovering, be sure to designate a large wall space for a bulletin board. (You might want to do this even if your walls will be plain.) Between two doors in a room can be a good spot, or on a bathroom or closet door, covered from the baseboard up to the top trim. In any case, select a generous area and glue Homasote in place so that your child's own art, treasures, and papers can be displayed. (Wallpaper can be too busy for displaying art.) Paint the bulletin board white or a contrasting color, or cover it with linen or felt.

Let Your Child Make Final Selections Let your child help in selecting the paper or vinyl. It is a mistake to assume that at this age a child won't have strong opinions.

FLOORS

The most important thing about the floor during this period—as it was in the previous one—is to have as much of it free for play as possible. The floor is still the most active surface in your child's room.

A smoothly sanded, natural-color hardwood floor with several coats of polyurethane for protection is still very practical because of the vigorous activity that will go on. The color of natural wood can be good because wood tones are restful. During these years of the most energetic play and wild inventiveness, a simple hardwood floor can be ideal.

Asbestos Vinyl   If you don't have a wood floor and need to install a floor covering, the least expensive vinyl is asbestos vinyl, which comes in a wide variety of textures and colors. Remember to experiment on a sample to be sure the vinyl will clean easily. (Run the black rubber from the heel of your child's shoe or the tire of one of his trucks on a tile sample and then wipe off the mark with a cleaning solution; this single experiment will tell you whether this surface can be cleaned easily.)

The floor in a child's place gets constant scraping and scratching, and, for this reason, a textured pattern, possibly with specks in similar colors, is safer than a solid-colored floor. Marks show less and the floor is easier to clean.

Area Rugs   Rugs that can be washed are an excellent way to break up the floor space.

WINDOWS

I still recommend white window frames, freshly painted. The window arrangement you decided on earlier may still be fine.

Shutters   If you've waited until now to decide on your window treatment, you might plunge into the investment of shutters. While expensive, they are clean, crisp, and no curtains or blinds are necessary. Shutters are screwed into your window trim, but legally they are yours when you sell a house or apartment, so you can take them with you when you move. Windows vary considerably, but usually shutters can be adapted to fit the windows in a new location.

Window Space   The area nearest the window should be developed because it connects the indoors to the out-of-doors and gives a room a sense of beyondness. Often, the window area becomes wasted space in a child's room because most furniture can't be put in front of a window. Also windows frequently have some kind of heating apparatus underneath them, and when two windows are next to each other, the radiator is often located in the center of the wall area in between. What can you do to utilize this space and not block light and heat?

1. *Window seat*   You can install a window seat relatively easily if you don't have a radiator that is too high and your windows are low enough so the ledge can become a replacement for the window sill. If your situation calls for it, a seat extending the entire length of the window wall could be useful. Install heavy angle irons approximately three feet apart for support and have the window seat approximately sixteen inches deep. A three-foot face on the front of the wood panel gives it a solid appearance and helps to hide any wires or heating units behind. Because dirt is unavoidable at a window area, use a laminated Formica for easier maintenance. Even if your child has to use a stool to get up to his seat, it will be used.

2. *Window-seat cushion*   To make a window-seat cushion, find a cotton material you like, buy a small swatch, measure it, and put it in the washing machine and dryer. Cotton shrinks and what you want to find out is whether you should buy a larger piece of material than is actually needed. (Wash it several times to preshrink it before you sew it onto your window-seat cushion.)

   Or, the cushion could be made of Dacron polyester, or of foam rubber 1½ to 2 inches high, zippered, or fastened with Velcro. Your child's stuffed animals, dolls, throw pillows, and miniature cars will be right at home here—as will your child.

3. *Window shelf*   If the bottoms of your windows are 26 inches from the floor and this is too high for a window seat, you might install a work counter under the window or windows. Same instructions as above but here you should put the shelf on top of the existing sill or remove the sill entirely to assure one continuous clean line.

4. *A sunken planter*   With an electric jigsaw, cut out from the window shelf a rectangle in the area closest to the window, and sink into this space a plastic planter.

5. *Window table on wheels for sand and water play*   For a completely portable solution to window space (and to create a great fun area for the child), buy or construct a sand-and-water play table to fit in front of the windows. If you have room for this kind of table in front of the windows, your child will have hundreds of hours of solid fun.

Community Playthings in Rifton, New York, makes an excellent piece of equipment for this—a table that is 2 feet by 4 feet and 22 inches high, with a top that can be added when block building is the order of the day. Inside this table is a plastic pan, six inches deep, with a drainage plug. (The plug allows you to drain the water out by having a small pan below without removing the larger pan.) In this enclosure finger painting, water and sand play, growing plants, doing soapy washes, blowing soap bubbles, working on a terrarium, building a fort, or making an animal farm can go on, safely.

LIGHTING

You need to have several different lighting possibilities. Every child is involved in fantasy and reality and needs to be able to set the proper stage, then change the mood. Lighting can do this. One high-powered blast of concentrated light coming from the ceiling might not be as useful for the child who is all over the place and involved in a variety of activities. Several less powerful lights might be a better solution. For example, if you have outlets on at least two walls you might have can wall lights which shoot light up and down. Traditional table lamps with shades take up precious surface space in the active playground, and you run the risk that they will get knocked over and possibly break. So, for work areas, a small Tensor lamp might be preferable. You can buy them so they either clip onto a table or shelf, or are wall mounted.

FURNITURE

Chances are that by the age of three, or thereabouts, your child has graduated into a standard-size bed, and you already have some storage pieces as basic equipment. For more information about beds, see chapters 3 and 7.

Earlier, much of the storage space was geared to parents' use. Now, this room should be prepared to be entirely turned over to the child and all the furniture and playthings geared for his imagination and growth. One thing to keep in mind about furniture is that the better it is designed and made for the child's own unsupervised use, the safer this child's place will be and the more completely independent the child can become in his own place, encouraging faster growth. Now you feel your child is starting to become an adult person, and the furniture system you and your child select represents the beginning of this independence.

Furniture Scale The average table height for children this age is 20 inches, with a 12-inch-high chair seat. Children love to work standing up, too, and the right height for a table to stand at is 26 to 28 inches. (This approaches adult table height for sitting—28 to 30 inches on the average—leading you into the proper height for sitting in the next age group, eight to thirteen.) Adult coffee tables average 16 to 18 inches in height, and you might find the table you buy or make now for your child could be used in his room, when he's older, as a coffee table or in other ways in years to come.

Table and Chair A table and chair should be introduced now as preparation for school; a child learns to feel comfortable sitting in a chair at a desk or table. Select a shape that suits the room size and the child's work needs. Have one low table for sitting and one higher for standing if the room is large enough. Changing positions is stimulating. To save space, the smaller table can be stored under the larger, higher one when it's not in use.

Make a Table At a lumberyard you can buy some sturdy legs that screw into your table top. The lumberyard will cut and bevel the edges of the table top smooth, to your dimensions. Consider laminated Formica for the top; it can easily be wiped clean after arts and crafts. Or, have a clear plastic disposable dropcloth handy to throw over the painted table, to avoid an accidental Jackson Pollack.

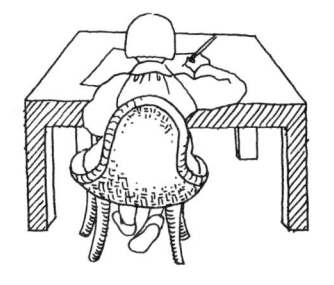

SPACE

Children slowly grow into a need for space and expansiveness. The small enclosed space of the infant enlarges now to a need for wide-open areas of empty space where the child can invent activity using playthings as props. These things should all be movable so the empty space itself stimulates the child into action.

Throughout this period, keep this space free from anything that isn't of current interest to the child. Children need space to be creative.

TEXTURES

Texture, design, and color are what soften, warm, and tie this multipurpose, action-packed room together. Your child gets attracted to certain blankets and particular animals and dolls. These soft, tactile things are what personalize and give security in their room. Contrasts fascinate children; they are extremely aware of the feel of everything in their world—the cool temperature of a table surface, the warm soft feel of a wool blanket, the cool wooden blocks, warm, soft soapy water, cool clay and sand, rough paper, the tickle of a brush, and smoothness of plastic—all are stimulating.

Texture Box Start a collection of small, brightly colored swatches and scraps of carpeting, materials, doilies, and wallpaper samples. Let your child pick some of them for his or her own box. Cover a brown carton with wrapping paper or a large piece of cotton. Put inside the box leaves, pebbles, shells, a feather, a rubber eraser, some cotton, some marbles. This texture box might become your child's first collection.

COLOR

Now your child's color preferences have begun to develop and he might really begin to establish a color combination in his room. This is an exciting time when colors are symbols and convey so many different things. They can establish the child's personal identity, his place.

Flexibility in Color A change of color to a child is a big change. Because it is an inexpensive form of change, it's a good idea to keep colors as flexible as possible. (One six-year-old girl protested that she is so sick of pink she could scream, but her bedroom is wallpapered in a pink ribbon design, with bedspread, headboard and curtains to match, so I don't think a color change is likely in Susanne's room for a long time.)

Choosing Designs and Colors   Color is greatly affected by the way it is used and its relationship to other colors. One of the charms of patchwork quilts is the use of so many varied and yet related patterns and color combinations. You and your child might decide to have several different patterns in the room, using colors to tie them together. When the basic background of a room is simple, colorful patterns can shine.

PLAYTHINGS

During bad weather, or in apartments, children need stimulating physical outlets; their room can double as a mini playground or gymnasium. Keep in mind that the room needs to encourage play.

BLOCKS

Blocks are universally used during childhood. Through blocks children can create and build their own world.

Block Storage   Blocks need plenty of storage space. A child spends a great deal of time constructing with blocks, and when finished playing, he should be encouraged to put them away neatly. You can aid by having a block storage space, and, if possible, try to provide separate sections for the various-sized blocks. Simply build some dividers into a large box so each block size and shape can be separated. This teaches size variations and dimensional differentiations to the child and also teaches the importance of caring for property. If a child is allowed to throw blocks in the bottom of a toy bin, the blocks get buried under other toys and scattered about. Community Playthings makes excellent blocks and also a 1-by-2-foot block cart, 15 inches high, on casters, with a shelf that slopes to the rear to encourage a child's good intentions!

INDOOR GYM

There are several gyms with slides for indoor use that are made commercially (as discussed in Chapter 3). I don't recommend making one unless you are really an experienced builder because a gym must be professionally constructed to be safe. But there are many on the market which you can easily assemble yourself. Buy a gym that can be folded or knocked down and put away when it's not in use.

ROCKING HORSE

Buy an old-fashioned rocking horse—the kind your grandparents played with when they were little—and plan to save it for your grandchildren! Rocking horses, just like rocking chairs, are always a prime attraction in a room.

ROCKING ROWBOAT

Community Playthings makes a rocking rowboat, big enough for your child and a friend. Turn it upside down and it doubles as a set of stairs! (Use as stairs until five years old, then turn over for a boat.)

DOMESTIC PLAY

Create a kitchen corner in your child's room. Many girls and boys love the idea of cooking, and all the domestic puttering needn't be restricted to your real kitchen. A child can use real ingredients, whip up things at his own work table, and then bake them in the adult kitchen. Rig up a cooking corner. Childcraft, Creative Playthings, and Community Playthings all sell housekeeping and kitchen furniture for children. Buy a sturdy wooden sink and stove unit with cupboards below. Or, you could make a sink by cutting a hole in the top of a plywood table and inserting a Rubbermaid bin! By adding a pair of spring hinges on the bottom of a door panel and a pull in the center, you have created an oven.

Put down a thin, clear, plastic dropcloth (the throw-away kind you can get in the paint store) when someone wants to cook, and give the children real materials to use. A five-year-old can shell peas, peel potatoes or carrots, stir Jell-O, and scramble eggs. They think it is much more fun than using fake foodstuff. A carrot peeler works beautifully (and is safe) on a block of cheese that needs shredding. Let your daughter make her own sandwiches, or even cookies for her birthday party. This preparation will be valuable later when you do cook together, and it makes your child feel important to have her own cooking place and equipment. ("You aren't the only one with a kitchen, Mom.") Scaled-down kitchen equipment can be stored in your child's room so that it is out of your way except when your child is baking or cooking. Even make-believe cookies and cakes made from colored clay can be lots of fun, only thing missing is the nibbling, the smells, and the licking!

LAUNDRY ROOM

Another use for this kitchen corner is as a laundry room. The "kitchen" sink instantly becomes an area for washing clothes. Put down the plastic dropcloth, put three inches of tepid water in the rubber pan, and give your child a sandwich-size baggie half full of Ivory Flakes. Buy a small washboard, and let your son, or daughter, scrub his own socks or sweater, or wash a doll's dress. I feel safer having this go on in an area scaled properly than in a bathroom where everything is adult size, hard, and slippery.

EASELS

An easel can be a functional, decorative, easy addition to a young person's room. Easels are handy because many children love to paint standing up. They come with holders for paints and brushes; some have blackboard backs. And when there isn't a painting in progress, there can be one on display. (You can display weather and topographical maps as well.) Put a clean canvas dropcloth under the easel and relax.

SCRAPBOOKS

Keep picture scrapbooks of children's rooms and show them to a child who is just beginning to express his own preferences. When you show a child a whole scrapbook filled with ideas that can be adapted and used for his own room, you help to open him up to express what he likes. Include all pictures you can gather of playthings. Some scrapbooks can be parent-child originated— another way of sharing. Let your child get the scrapbook habit early; it's fun to cut out pictures and paste them in scrapbooks.

Beyond the Basics

1. *On one of your child's four white walls,* one day grow a tree or a flower garden. Paint with acrylic paints—green, red, yellow, and brown—and paint over your penciled-in outline. If you want to change your design, erase away the pencil with "Fantastic" or another cleaner. If you want to remove the design entirely, paint over it with white Emalj after it has dried.

2. *Paint a game design right on your child's floor.*   Or, paint on the floor the symbols of children's games. You might paint a colorful tic-tac-toe, or a hopscotch, or a checkerboard in primary six-inch squares.

3. *Build a loft inside the closet.*   Have a sturdy wooden ladder made at the lumberyard and construct solid boards across the top area 30 or 36 inches from the ceiling. The ladder should hook onto a two-inch lip around the top edge for safety. This "child's place" is a hiding place and a special place to play alone or with a friend. Depending on the age and co-ordination of your child, supervision until approximately six years will probably be required.

4. *Make a half-round iron canopy for your daughter's bed,* or ask a craftsman to do so. Paint it white and shirr a two-sided cotton material into a ruffled edge. Attach it with Velcro so it can easily be removed for washing.

Our oldest daughter shares bunk beds with her sister, and she wanted a roof over her head the way her sister had in the lower bunk. Our ceilings are 10 feet high, so we were able to put a canopy on the top bunk. We selected a sun-yellow cotton with tiny white polka dots. So that the child below in the bottom bed wouldn't feel left out, we covered her "roof" (which in fact is the mattress and springs supporting the upper bed) with a piece of the same yellow cotton polka-dot material, shirred on a rod. A great warm feeling when lying on your back in bed!

5. *Buy your child an exercise mat* made to fit the floor under the doorway, then hang a swing in the doorway. Child Life Play Specialties, Inc., sells both in a variety of solid colors.

6. *Buy a doorway gym* with a swing, trapeze bar, and trapeze rings. (Child Life Play Specialties, Inc.)

7. *Add a bed frame* to your child's bed, raising the bed for sleeping to the top, like a bunk bed. Keep the bottom bare, add canvas flaps that can be closed or opened and tied back. Scandinavian Designs, Inc., created this idea and sells a lot of beds set up this way. Eventually a frame can be added for a friend spending the night or for a sister or brother. For now, a castle, a fort, and a single bunk bed on top.

8. *Make a place to romp.* If you have an extra king- or queen-size bed and don't have room to store it, or don't want to pay to put it in storage, and if there is enough room, use it in your child's room as a place to romp. Remove the Harvard frame and put the box spring and mattress right on the floor in a corner. Even in a small room where this would take up most of the floor space, it can be fun for romping and jumping, which goes on anyway with small children. So why not have a place where it will be safe and padded so the noise level, from your neighbor's viewpoint, isn't too nerve-racking. This large surface is ideal for friends sleeping over. It's there and ready to catch the sleepy children as they fall.

Chapter 5

GROWING OUT

(ages eight to thirteen)

SOLITUDE
I have a house where I go when there's
too many people.
I have a house where I go where nobody
ever says "No";
Where no one says anything—so
There is no one but me.

Now We Are Six
by A. A. MILNE

When I was at home I was in a better place.

As You Like It
Act II
Scene IV
WILLIAM SHAKESPEARE

GROWING UP

Experts say that a child's personality, character creativity, and academic motivation are 80 per cent accomplished by his or her eighth year. By that time he is able to make a clear distinction between work and play—work is work and play is play.

Once a child understands about work, she needs a room that provides her with work space, as well as play space. It's important for children to understand this distinction, as this realization is one of the steps toward an adult pattern of life.

Because of this, in this chapter one of the main things we'll focus on, in particular, is outlining ways of adapting your child's room to combine play areas (social areas) with areas for study and quiet. Adults often have separate rooms for sleeping, eating, working, and entertaining; begin when a child is eight or so to give him a variety of these options, in his one room.

Aside from the work/play necessity, the design can be similar in many ways to the period before.

Just as the school experience is meant to support the home environment, the home should also support the school experience. The goals are the same. Provide uncluttered surfaces for your child to work on as well as play. One of your primary goals should be to see that the room presents a spirit of readiness. It should have areas for work and play and also should be welcoming and invite a flood of activity.

FURNITURE PLAN

In the previous chapter, the room resembled a playroom with lots of clear space for movement and action. Now the child will be dividing his time between home and school, so structure and form become important. Order is essential, and it's wise to have a set plan for the arrangement of the furniture. A place for everything allows the child the chance to put things away and always know exactly where supplies and materials are.

If possible, the desk area should be a special place, clear and ready for homework. The bed no longer doubles only as a play place, but also becomes a place on which to flop down during quiet times and to read on. There should be work surfaces for important school materials, a clean place to study, and space for work in progress.

A private corner to play in and be with a friend or two, a place for the magic table or play stage, is also a necessity. The loft on top of the closet is loved by children at this age as a private retreat, a place to read. The top of a bunk bed might be turned into a place up away from things. A place with pillows, to climb to and read. But mainly, a place designed for work, as well as places for play, is what's important now.

SCALE

During his eight-to-thirteen age period a child is approaching the scale of adults. The 26 to 28 inch high table used for standing at by the younger child may now be the right height for sitting at, with a 17- to 18-inch high chair. Heights take on increased importance because the room is no longer a play area but a place where studying and concentrated work are also done. Scale and proportions are vital design considerations during these important growth years because this one room has to be an everything and should be divided up into as many areas as possible and as required, depending on the personality of your child.

One last word on scale for the eight-to-thirteen age group. Your child might be a foot taller than another child at his same age. Late bloomers or early bloomers, each child grows at his own rate. The child who is on the tall side for his age could be sensitive because he or she is bigger than others in the class. The small child who hasn't started to sprout may be unfairly affected by the great emphasis on size, especially if the child is a boy. Know your child and take his sensitivities into consideration. Be sure his feet touch the floor on the swivel chair. Keep in mind to study the child's true dimensions, periodically—not what is average size for his age group. Keep the scale flexible, as much as possible. Your child's growth will determine how the scale should grow.

COLOR

Many children between the ages of eight to thirteen will develop strong attachments to certain colors and color combinations and grow into new appreciation of specific colors, sometimes almost overnight. The emotion-evoking and aesthetic impact of color is strong during this stage of becoming more grownup and individual. Color sense, and therefore choice of colors, becomes more subtle, and there is a recognition of shades: the crayon-box primary colors of red, yellow, blue, green might turn to more sophisticated shades of salmon, pistachio, lavender, tomato, and maroon. Because the child may move quickly through preferences for different tones and combinations, the colors in his room should be kept as flexible as possible. For instance, if his current color choice is turquoise or another exciting color, use it to stripe a bookcase, or for the door trim, or spray-paint it onto a tin wastebasket. Then, when the child's preference changes from turquoise to indigo blue, you don't have to redo the entire room. Often, the old color favorite fits in, in small doses, with a newer color interest. The effect of yesterday's purple and pink is changed by the addition of yellow and peach.

A CHILD'S WORK OF ART

The most significant color story at this age is the child's own color expression through his art. A younger child might have done a quick painting but now a work of art may be concentrated on for hours. This might represent a large block of time and lots of feeling—a statement. The colors and the way they're combined in a child's work of art might suggest a scheme for his or her room.

Buy inexpensive clear plastic frames (they come in a wide selection of sizes), and frame one of these paintings to hang over your child's desk, or on the wall nearest his bed. This will personalize the room and help make the child feel more grown up. A child's color sense can be fresh, innocent, and effective.

Or, take your child to a museum with you and let him pick out a colorful poster. What could be better than having a master artist's work on his white wall, to stare at and imagine with?

WALLS

A child's collection of knickknacks and cherished small objects continues to grow. The wall can display some of these things, safely. Hanging shelves, a rack, or a set of corner shelves are good additions to a child's place; hang them at the eye level of the standing child so they are handy as well as decorative. This is the age when the child becomes attached to small things which are not toys but articles, often breakable and part of what might become a growing collection. If you buy a few hanging shelves, of wicker, plastic, or wood, you will probably see them used and filled in a short time. Dickens characters; Beatrix Potter animals; china animal miniatures; model airplanes; miniature trains; cars and trucks; shells; rocks; clay and plaster creatures, and framed photographs of family and friends—all need housing and should not interfere with study space or hobby space. Separate these collections by displaying them on shelves on the wall.

The wall can also function as a place to paint, house a Murphy bed, become an entire floor-to-ceiling storage unit or a drop-down Formica work counter. Because there is such an increase in the functional needs in the room as the child develops new outside interests and skills, the walls can be put to use to store wanted items and created needed storage space and work areas. Take a good look at the wall space available for use in your child's place, and see if you are using it as effectively as you might.

WINDOWS

Window Box   Your son or daughter might be a budding horticulturalist and the window area can now become the child's own garden. By installing plant-grow lights at the top of the window and hanging shelves approximately twelve inches apart, you have a simple, good beginning. If there is a radiator under the window area, build an insulated shelf over the unit and have a window box with a generous layer of pebbles on the bottom to provide good drainage for the pots of greenery and to keep the window area moist.

If the window frames a good view, be sure the bed or sitting area takes advantage of it.

Depending on the dimensions of the room, it might be a good idea to place the bed parallel to the window, at about two feet from it. This can be a particularly good setup when the bed is either a bunk bed or a canopy bed because the height makes the window part of the bed unit.

Curtains Inexpensive, washable curtains hung and possibly tied back can add a necessary softness, especially if you have a daughter. Cafe curtains, which can be pulled closed at night, are good for a boy's or a girl's room. If you installed shutters earlier, they'll still be ideal.

FLOOR

At this age, and in the periods to come, the floor space will increasingly be broken up with furniture; also, the floor won't be used so constantly for play and building. Therefore, carpeting may now be a good alternative solution to bare floors. Wall-to-wall carpeting, while more expensive, has the advantage in that it ties the whole space together.

Carpeting A flat, tightly woven carpeting is the most practical. Watch out for synthetics in light tones, and keep in mind that the higher the pile, the more static electricity will attract dirt. Spots may come clean, but then the rest of the carpet may look gray in contrast. A low loop-pile carpet is preferable, and one with a few shades of one color (for instance, shades of green or tones of blue or beige) would be a good practical choice. Indoor-outdoor carpeting comes in a big selection now, is relatively low in cost, and is easy to keep up. If you can afford wool carpeting, it will last long and clean well.

Rubber Backing There are many kinds of inexpensive synthetic carpeting on the market which are rubber backed and can be glued to the floor. Avoid gluing carpeting to a good wood floor, however, because the carpet can be difficult to remove, and you will probably have to scrape the wood floor to get all the glue up—a messy job! If you're going to use a rubber backed carpeting, tack it down at the edges, instead of using glue.

Wood If you have a nice wood floor, and you'd like to keep the floor bare, add a small, fluffy shag rug near the bed and another one in the sitting area. These rugs can be purchased inexpensively in bath shops. Area rugs can also be used to divide up the room into different areas—one small rug to define the work area, another to define the sleep area, etc.

Your son or daughter might like to help you hook a sunburst rug or possibly make a small needlepoint rug for the room. A 2-by-4 foot should be large enough to add a feeling of warmth and color and yet be small enough not to take forever to complete.

FABRICS AND TEXTURES

Children in this period of growth move forward toward independence while clinging to aspects of their earlier self. Preferred dolls, animals, Snoopy, teddy bears, favorite blankets, sleeping bags, and pillows are still necessary companions. Boys are no exception to this sentimental attachment. An old blanket worn thin and threadbare might be just the touch of security he needs, at the foot of the bed. The affection for these objects makes the room live and can help keep the child from feeling lonely.

Certain colors and textures stimulate a child, so take your son with you when you buy bath towels to use in his bathroom. If you find several colors and designs on sale, have him select from the sales group. Do the same when buying sheets and blankets. Making these choices automatically heightens enjoyment and gives the child a strong feeling of self.

Go into the linen closet with your child from time to time and see if there is something that catches his eye. Often an old set of sheets or a familiar pillowcase or blanket will be most welcome again. The memory of the old and familiar is a form of roots.

ACCESSORIES

By now this one room has decidedly taken on the personality of the child. Just as the adult acquires, accumulates, collects, and gathers, so does the child. The old, broken toys, the puzzle with missing pieces, dried-up paint tubes, and scraps of clay can be thrown out. The real things remain: a post card or baseball-card collection in a show box, books, an animal scrapbook, paintings, stories, poems, old favorite dolls and animals, collections of miniatures, stamps, coins, a costume box, easel, magic equipment, stationery, and art supplies.

MAINTENANCE

The room is easier to keep orderly now than in earlier periods because it has a more fixed arrangement. Many children at this age thrive on accomplishment; if the child is not capable of caring for his own possessions now, good habits may be difficult to establish later on. Children at this age have so many interests and are so active in this multipurpose room that neatness is necessary and inspires a child the way a clean kitchen does a cook. Try to set things up so that everything has a place, and let your child help maintain it.

A PLACE TO COME HOME TO

When your child goes to school, he begins to develop not only patterns of work, but also peer friendships which become important. Instead of having a room all to himself or a room to share with a brother or sister, children in school share a common room with many other boys and girls. You will notice how your young school-age child enjoys her own room when she arrives home from school. The fact that her room is waiting for her is security in itself. Happiness is having a child's place to come home to.

HAVING FRIENDS OVER

Of course a child doesn't grow and develop solely within the restrictions of one room's dimensions or space allotment. Once your child has daily exposure at school to group activities and interaction with peers, he will quickly discover the fun of having friends over. At first, it is often easier for a child to invite friends over than it is to be a guest in a friend's unfamiliar room. A child, left alone, will automatically act as host or hostess; he or she will screen friends, inviting over those who have a lot in common. In the selection of a particular friend, your child is saying, "I trust Christopher to come into my home and into my room and not steal my Snoopy or my Life Savers; or break my mobile; or spill paint on my science experiment; or write stupid things in my favorite book; or irritate my mother so she raises her voice and seems angry all afternoon."

The room plays an important role because it has to do with the child's identity. "This is where I live. This is my room. This is my table, piano, my books. I'd like to share them with you." The more a friend enjoys a child's room, the more the child respects what is there.

This early socializing, especially if a child doesn't have several siblings, is important; the room continues to be the stage for the child's activities and development. So in planning the room with a child of this age, provide for lots of different kinds of areas. He should be able to play all acts out here, without a change of scene. Disposable plastic or canvas dropcloths can be kept handy for times when a project is about to begin. Store these right in the child's closet. All accidents can be easily cleaned up by the children. Make this a place for spontaneity.

THE COZY CORNER

Another thing to plan for, as mentioned earlier, might be a cozy reading corner where the child can cuddle up and read right on the floor. It might have a soft-textured, inviting area rug (a high-pile, loosely woven shag might be a good device), or even a thin mattress covered in a soft-to-the-touch fabric (corduroy or cotton velvet or angora), with lots of floppy pillows to snuggle into and curl up on while reading. This corner should have some kind of a throw, either a quilt or an afghan or a wooly blanket that can be draped around the child for the feeling of warmth while reading. Beanbag chairs can also be good for this reading corner. They allow the child to flop down and get into a comfortable position. A small Tensor light hung on the wall provides good concentrated light. This area should have an enclosed feeling, a feeling of privacy, and one way to do this could be by framing a "barricade"—two low bookcases at right angles out into the room.

BOOKCASES

An inviting way to display books is to have slanted shelves (with a lip on the bottom of the shelf so the books won't fall off). This way, the book jacket is visible and can stimulate the young reader and capture his attention. In sight, in mind. Childcraft makes bookcases like this in clear maple.

Books are busy, so when painting bookcases I'd suggest you stick to white frames; you might use your accent color as striping around the edges and inside the shelves and on the back for an added touch of stimulation. White shows off the books and reflects light, making the books appear more vivid to the child.

If your room is large enough, you could put two low units back to back—one facing the reading corner filled with books and the other facing the bed or desk area with some books and some space to display a collection or to store supplies. If this double arrangement isn't suited to your child's room, why not glue some colorful heavy felt on the back of a bookcase (book side faces the reading corner) so the back, which is facing out into the room, can be a display area for your child? Felt shapes stick to felt, so this can be a safe form of entertainment, a kind of substitute drawing board, for younger children. Or, for an older child, glue to the back of a bookcase some Homasote (the insulating material that comes in sheets and can easily be cut to size). It can be painted or covered over with felt or linen, and your child can make designs with colored pushpins. Or, cover the entire back surface with a magnetic board and/or a blackboard.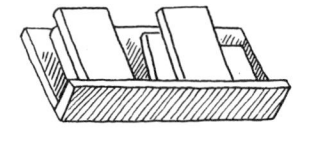

Childcraft makes a bookcase with two wings hinged together, one wing with adjustable shelves for flat display of books and one designed for spine display of books. This is. ideal to put in a corner to give the room, or corner, a library feeling. Add a soft, shaggy area rug.

One mother turned two bookcases on their sides to convert a tall vertical bookcase into a low horizontal one. Her two daughters shared a room and each had one bookcase. The bookcases were arranged at right angles; Karen's was against a wall and Emily's unit came out into the room, creating a small divider. Her book side could not be seen from Karen's side because Emily's was turned around with the back adjoining Karen's. Karen had privacy, Emily had privacy; by reversing the front of one bookcase, each girl had her own little place. Emily had one section as a stable for horses, and her father put in a divider in each shelf making a series of square cubbyholes just right for books, puzzles, games, and display area. (The backs of these cubbies could be painted different colors, too.)

BASIC FURNITURE

A bed, a desk, and a chair are now the most basic furniture elements in your child's place.

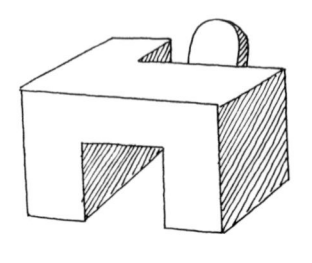

Desk   A desk arrangement should be set up now, if there isn't one already, so your child will learn to feel comfortable sitting in a chair, at a desk. It helps a child develop good work habits. Learning how to sit still at a desk and concentrate can be a valuable education. A desk can be a special place to your child; it depends on the way you present it. All kinds of creative energy can be expressed and put to use while sitting at a desk; also, it teaches order to a child.

Selecting a desk that your child really likes will make a big difference in how much it gets used. What kind would your child enjoy the best? Gather pictures of as many models as you can find and look them over with your child, and when you're out together, notice different desk shapes. Before you actually go to buy a desk, know what type your child would like most.

Does your child like wood? Or is color or design more important? You will find your child will be developing definite preferences in style and design and this first desk, while not something that has to last forever, represents a big decision. I don't recommend spending a lot of money to buy a child's fancy desk. There are many inexpensive ways to approach the desk problem (we'll discuss some shortly), but, basically, keep in mind that a desk is a place where your child can go to write and read.

By looking around and exploring all kinds of possibilities, you will be able to find a desk arrangement your child will be happy with. An old wooden desk from the Salvation Army, with the legs cut shorter, may be just right for now. I know a nine-year-old who has his heart set on a rolltop desk. Your child will certainly be fascinated to go to a parent's office and see his or her desk. Once your child learns to type, a typewriter arm might be added on as a handy addition to the desk. You can buy a small steel secretary's desk reasonably at a furniture supply company. Watch for ads in your newspaper or check the Yellow Pages.

Your child's desk is individual. It isn't the fact that your child needs to use the desk at one particular moment, it is more that the desk is there, waiting. . . . The emotional space it represents is stronger than physical square feet. For this reason, a table and chair used as a substitute for a rectangular desk isn't necessarily the best solution; if you can only have one or the other, I'd recommend the desk.

A Desk Complex You might take your child to Childcraft to see their latest "absorption center for peace of mind—a desk complex for a child." They sell an Italian-designed high piece which has a blackboard as a work-play surface and hideaway stools which are stored inside.

Or, take your eight-year-old to Children's Workbench to see its adjustable desk from Finland. This desk is a sturdy construction in pine, and the top is a durable gray linoleum. It can be adjusted to be anywhere from 24 to 32 inches high (the adjustments can be made at two-inch intervals), so your child can use this desk forever. The large 47-by-30-inch surface can be used as a drawing board or a worktable (with a cloth over it, this could eventually double as a dining table), and it can be a great place for friends to sit when you have a party. I know an eleven-year-old who has been using this desk complex; Sam is an illustrator and he has his desk adjusted on a slant so the back pins are higher than the pins in front.

The Children's Workbench also sells a three-drawer pedestal to go with this desk; it can go underneath or be used as a separate unit. This desk is designed for action and wears well with continuous use.

Kneehole Desk Your child might prefer a kneehole desk. You can put together this kind of desk, with drawers on either side, by buying two 15-inch chests (such as the Muurame model) and adding a piece of wood for the top. This is one of the most practical desk arrangements because it is so flexible. (Like military desks, it is made in sections so it can be easily transported, or used in flexible arrangements.)

Formica Desk A plywood or Formica board, supported by two cubes, can be used to create another good desk solution. The cubes might be red, blue, or yellow plastic, and the top board might be painted to match. This could provide you with a desk for under $30 that would last until you and your child decide to go into something more substantial. The rectangular shape should be the goal. Ten-cent stores now carry plastic cubes with open shelves as well as cubes with doors and drawers. Orange crates can be painted and used, as well as painted frozen orange juice cans and coffee cans for holding pencils, Magic Markers, and crayons. You can have a lumberyard make you some low wooden sawhorses with a board on top which would be easy to move around. For storage, you could go to an art supply store and get a plastic drawer unit on casters. Also Childcraft makes a brick-finish table-desk with a white laminated plastic surface; impervious to paint and crayon marks, it resists scratches and dents. This sturdy little rectangular table comes in a variety of sizes.

Wooden Desk   Wood is becoming scarce today, and with the new materials available there are lots of alternatives to wood; but an old-fashioned wooden desk might be appreciated the most by your child. If you love antiques and have an antique desk you want to put in your child's room, be sure you have a good understanding with your child as to the rules of maintaining it. No matter how much it would please you, I don't recommend putting an antique in your child's room if your child does not at this stage want the responsibility of caring for a valuable piece of furniture. An old dressing table painted white and striped with yellow or blue or pink might be more appreciated than an antique pine desk which your child doesn't want to have to worry about.

Schoolroom Furniture   Inquire at your school and see if they know where you can purchase used schoolroom furniture. An old schoolroom desk could be useful, familiar, and just the right size.

Now that many schools have done away with the old-fashioned rows of desks which were bolted to the floor, those desks have become fascinating to young children. If you can find one that has a writing arm and slanted top on a hinge, your child might have some fun with it. Bolt this to the floor near a window.

Placement of a Desk   Try to place the desk in a sunny place—if possible, near a window. Try to avoid a dark corner, and try not to have it too close to the door. Rather, place it so your child can see the door from where he or she sits. Don't build in a desk unless it is part of a wall unit which can be moved around.

DESK CHAIR

The seat of a desk chair should be ten inches lower than the ideal height of the desk. If the desk is 26 inches high, the chair seat should be 16 inches. Children often sit on their knees, so be sure the seat isn't scratchy or too hard. If the chair has a rush seat, put a cushion on it. A desk chair should have a straight back.

Childcraft and Creative Playthings, Inc., make a solid-beech side chair in different heights. (A low desk chair, once outgrown, might be fun in the reading corner.)

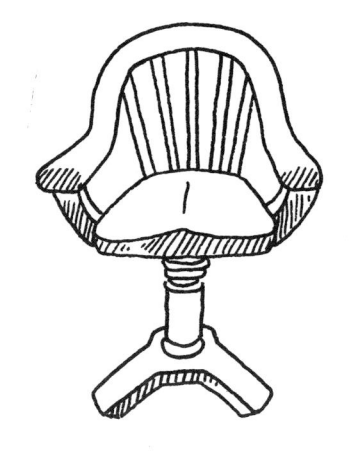

Swivel Chair   Children all love to swivel. If you can find an inexpensive swivel chair, add it to the child's place. The Children's Workbench makes a swivel chair on casters which adjusts to several heights; it comes in a choice of primary colors.

Side Chair   When your child is big enough to sit at a regular 18-inch-high seat, you might consider investing in a Saarinen Tulip chair in white plastic with a colored vinyl seat cushion. These chairs are easy to care for and can last a lifetime.

Another desk chair, without a swivel, is the bentwood chair (also known as an ice cream parlor chair). Design Research makes these in a natural finish or in colors. Unpainted-furniture stores also carry them.

If your son has seen his father's leather office chair that swivels and tilts, he might want a barrel, pedestal desk chair on casters. There are many office chairs, reasonable in cost, which are small in scale, adjustable in height, and can be covered in a colored washable vinyl. Inquire at your local department store or office supply company. (Don't forget that the Yellow Pages often give helpful clues to useful sources; and while we're on the subject of telephone books, if your child has a chair which is a bit too low for his new desk, a year-old phone book or a foam-rubber cushion covered in a lively fabric could add four inches to the seat height!)

SPACE FOR WORK IN PROGRESS: THE WORK AREA

Every adult knows how difficult it is to be in the middle of a project and have to put it away abruptly, out of sight. Somehow the creative urge gets folded up with the supplies. The most frequent complaint I hear as a decorator is that people don't have a place where they can leave projects out, to come back to. See if you can find a place in your child's place for hobbies and work in progress. A puzzle with a lot of pieces can't be put back in the box every time there is an interruption.

Where in the room is the best place to have projects in work?

The floor is a perfect place for all kinds of play; games and toys can be enjoyed while the child sits and flops on the floor. Or the desk—it should be relatively uncluttered so your child can go and sit at it to read or write a letter or do a homework assignment without having to move other things out of the way.

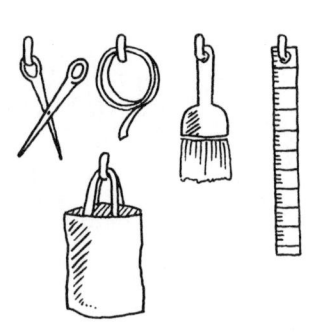

Work and hobby projects should have their own separate places. Establish where this space will be located in your child's room and organize it so that surface space and storage space are close together. Plan thoughtfully an uncluttered surface where your child can resume work; this will definitely stimulate development of extra projects. Provide storage areas for all the tools required; materials and supplies should be at arm's length so that glue, brushes, scissors, markers, Scotch tape, paints are close at hand.

MAKE A HIGH PLACE

Height can be used to separate work areas from play areas. Plan a wall of shelf space with a laminated Formica top which is high up enough to sit at with a stool. For the stool, you could use an unpainted wooden stool from a hardware store, or you can use a kitchen stool which has steps for reaching supplies on high shelves. Or, buy a swivel bar-type stool. An adjustable stool is especially useful since your child can change the height when he wishes.

The bottom of the Formica work shelf should be 7 to 10 inches above the top of the stool; or let the shelf be adjustable, too.

SHELVES

Standards and Brackets   In order to create shelves that are adjustable, use standards with brackets. In any hardware store you can buy wall standards—metal strips that are installed vertically on the wall; the brackets are inserted at intervals on the standards, and the brackets hold the shelves. If you want to change the height of a shelf, you just move the brackets up or down a notch to another position. Even though the standards and brackets are metal, they come in a wide variety of finishes—black, white, wood-grained, satin or bronze finish, or they can be painted the color of the wall to make them less noticeable. Your local hardware store will probably stock ¾-inch-thick shelves in three lengths, 24, 36, and 48 inches and two widths, 8 and 10 inches. You should plan to have a bracket every 30 inches, to avoid overloading a shelf without proper support.

To make some shelves deeper than others, all you have to do is buy a bigger, larger bracket and wider board. The most often used bracket sizes are 6 to 14 inches deep but you can purchase them from as small as 4 inches deep up to 18 inches. A shelf with brackets 18 inches deep uses a heavier weight standard and makes an excellent desk-work area.

Shelves Above the Work Area Above the work area can be narrow six- or eight-inch shelves for displaying a collection or for supplies and books which you want in a safe place, yet nearby.

To save space, you may decide that you want narrow shelves, plus one deeper shelf on a hinge so that when it's not in use it can be folded down, where it won't take up space.

WALL-MOUNTED WORK AREA

The wall-mounted work area can be put up at any point during your child's development. When your baby is on the floor crawling around, there could be low shelves with soft rubber bins for toys and blocks in reach—later to become a work area for special projects.

LIGHTING THE WORK AREA

Wall lights with a swing arm or gooseneck are ideal for a work area. Art supply stores sell inexpensive wall lights in bright primary colors. Also, there are clamp-on lights which are a simplified version of the classic architect's lamp. Try to avoid a lamp and shade that take up surface space, as this interrupts the flow of work in the area. Concentrated light over a work area encourages a child to hone in on work at hand.

Another inexpensive and easy solution is to install a strip of fluorescent lighting under an upper shelf. If you decide to use fluorescent lighting here, be sure to buy daylight bulbs which attempt to imitate natural daylight.

Also, a Tensor lamp might be a good solution; they are tiny, adjustable, and powerful.

This high-up work area should be a private place, if possible— not disturbed by parents or baby sitters—because it is your child's important work area.

STORAGE ON THE DESK OR WALL WORK AREA

Colored plastic storage bins can be labeled and used in this area. The labels save your child from reaching for the wrong bin. Or, buy clear-plastic shoe or sweater boxes so your child can see inside. If a more elaborate storage wall is planned, be sure to have many open shelves where colored storage cubes will fit right in. They can be quickly removed, worked with, and returned to order in seconds.

Metal Bookcase   A wonderful storage solution for games, hobbies, and supplies is a metal bookcase from an office supply store. Nothing is stronger, or cheaper, and it probably can be delivered to your door faster than one purchased at a furniture store. Unfortunately, your local supply house may not have the brightly colored ones in stock. If you get one in the standard battleship gray (you might find one secondhand), spray or paint it with an enamel paint in a cheerful color. They are so practical you'll want them for other storage needs around the house. Paint it the same color as one of the colors of the plastic bins you plan to use. Even if you plan to have closed storage cabinets, you might find metal bookcases a good storage idea for inside closets.

Plastic Shelves   Another good storage idea for on top of a desk is colored plastic shelves. You can buy matching components for ends and separatives; they click into each other and when combined, they form stacked shelving. You can assemble your own unit as you wish. These units come apart when you want to move them into a new arrangement or into another room or house. They are amazingly sturdy, even though they are lightweight and inexpensive.

SLEEPING OVER

Most of us are short of space; people are forced to live with less space than ever before. So it can be difficult to find room for your children's friends who want to sleep over. Children don't care if their friends have adult guest-room accommodations or elaborate sleeping quarters when they sleep over; the whole point of sleeping over is to have a good time, to be goofy, a little devilish, to be silly, and to sleep in an unfamiliar place. And, most important, to be together. Anticipate these nights and plan several possible sleep-over arrangements, then let the children pick which one they'd like best. The less formally you plan each event, the better.

The Floor as a Bed Young children instinctively use the floor for curling up and napping. A child will sleep on the floor on a hot summer night because it is the coolest and, therefore, the most comfortable spot. Until an adult tells a child to get off the floor, that's where he instinctively likes to be.

For a sleep-over, put a clean sheet over an area rug, to create a territory, an island on the floor. Then buy or make snuggly sleeping bags for slumber parties or overnight friends. A 68-inch-square quilt can be zippered into a sleeping bag. Or, find two quilted throws reasonably priced, and put them together for a sleeping bag, by using Velcro, or snap tape, or a zipper. Check in your local department store in their children's sleepwear section for lightweight sleeping bags in a print your child likes.

When a child has a friend over to spend the night, you can't put the friend in your child's bed and relegate your child to the floor in a sleeping bag; when they both have the same sleeping arrangement, then that's when it's special.

The Extra Bed Another solution is to keep a single mattress under the bed, covered with a colorful vinyl material so it can be wiped clean easily. When you have more than two young children spending the night together, use this low floor mattress.

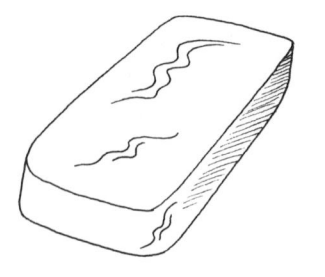

If you have a sofa bed, you might consider putting it in your child's room for your child and his or her friends to use.

Or a child may want two single beds set up all the time. They can be used daily as an extra place to sit and lounge, as well as for guests sleeping over. To diminish the depth, use bolsters or regular sleeping pillows, slipcovered. Your spare bed, used as a daybed against the wall, can create a warm sitting-room feeling —instead of taking up floor space by jutting out into the room.

Trundle Beds   Many trundle beds can be raised to the level of the bed next to it. Children's Workbench makes a trundle bed which slides out and stays low. This is good as a safe spare bed for small children.

MUSIC

Piano   If you have a piano and your child is the only one who plays it, keeping it in the living room may not be the best solution. If you are having friends in for the afternoon while your child is practicing, or having a lesson, it poses a conflict. Why not consider keeping the piano in the child's room?

An upright piano takes up the least amount of space. You might be able to get one secondhand. If the dark brown wood doesn't add life to your child's place, you could spray-paint it a bright color. If you buy a new upright, look into light finishes so the piano won't appear too dark and heavy in the room.

Record Players   Music is a large part of your child's life. So much of the music played and listened to by a child would not necessarily be your choice, so consider encouraging this interest by providing for it in your child's place. Record players aren't expensive and they are easy for a child to use. Children learn to care for records just as they do for books. Keep the ones they like accessible.

Musical Instruments   If you have a musically gifted child, you will probably discover this talent early.

If you do, try to create a room arrangement that allows space for practice—to set up drums, or to sit and play the clarinet or violin. There should be a safe place to store small instruments. When possible, let this space be open so that the instruments will be in sight. When the eye sees them—music begins. My children once received a small child's table piano; we put it on a low table with a chair and set up a place for the songbook with notes by color; this little piano was constantly in use. If it had been stored away on a shelf behind closed doors, it would have seemed like work to get it out, and I'm sure it would have been used less.

Stimulate your child's love of music. Hang tambourines on the wall; or hang a triangle on a hook from the ceiling so your child can lie in bed and create beautiful notes. Heighten your child's sense of sound by having bells on the door to make music every time the door is opened or closed. Hang some chimes near a window. Allow your child to play the harmonica or the record player when he's in bed. Hang the banjo or guitar on the wall near the bed. There, it is always handy and ready to be played.

BIKES, SKIS, AND SURFBOARDS

No longer do we all have mud rooms for hockey sticks and baseball mitts and golf clubs and snorkeling gear. The front-hall closet is already full of coats and hats, and it's really not the place for golf clubs and tennis rackets. Your child should be responsible for his own possessions and, whenever possible, store them in his own child's place. Helmets, mitts, skis, and surfboards should be cared for and safe in your child's own area. This way, no one else can be blamed when something is missing or warped or scratched.

Bikes or other large pieces of equipment are difficult to store in a bedroom, but it can be done. If you live in an apartment building without a bike room, and your child's room is too small to stand it against the wall taking up floor space, the bike could be hung on the wall on metal angle irons. Or, hang heavy chains from the ceiling and hook the tires on the chains. Have the bike as close to a wall as possible, but off the floor.

A surfboard could also hang on the wall on wooden brackets.

For skis, find a wall either inside your child's closet or inside his closed storage area. Tie the skis together with straps or thick elastic bands and install on the wall four-inch wood pegs a few inches apart—eight inches from the top of the skis and eight inches from the bottom. Put elastic across these pegs to hold the skis in place, or buy a metal clip to hold them securely.

Ice skates should be tied together, protected with rubber on

the blades, and stored off the floor, too. Hang them on a hook in the closet. (It's safer than storing them on a high shelf, where they could cut a child if they fell.)

A pegboard is good for the storage wall in a closed storage area. Hang the pegboard about eleven inches off the floor. Baseball mitts can be hung up on it, as well as boxing gloves, fishing rods, hockey sticks, tennis rackets in their frames. A baseball bat should be hung up and secured in place with elastic or a clamp —the way you would keep a broom or mop in place. Inquire at your hardware store as to what kinds of clamps you can buy and install them for all this gear. Just as your broom closet keeps all the household cleaning equipment together, I suggest your child's place have one closed storage section for sporting equipment. You can have hooks and shelves for helmets, sweatshirts, jogging pants, parkas, tackle box, tennis balls, Frisbees, hiking boots, and footballs. When tennis clothes come out of the dryer, they should be put back on a shelf in this area. Having these things all together in an orderly storage place leaves more time for study and play.

DANCING

Your child is learning new things at school each day and will want to continue these new interests at home. For example, your daughter might love to dance. If she studies dancing at school, or at a private dancing class, consider finding a brass bar and installing it in her room with a mirror above it. Even a towel bar could serve the same purpose. You could buy mirror glass in twelve-inch squares and put them up yourself. Home practice in the privacy of a child's place might be especially rewarding. Childcraft has a nice triptych mirror which can be moved around—another alternative.

ACTIVITIES AND GAMES

Backgammon or typing or recording or weaving—all are experiences that teach your child who she is, what she likes, who she will grow to become. No one is gifted at everything, but exposure to a variety of activities gives the child the chance to find out what his talents are. For some it will be art or music, for others it will be hand work or computers or sports or inventions. Try to make available in your child's place, at this stage, as many of these interests as you can, to help the child develop and continue developing. Quietly and with love you can add great perspective and dimensions to your child in this child's place.

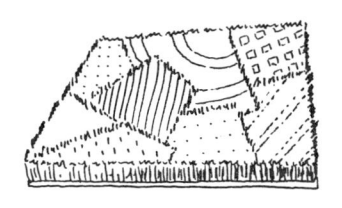

Beyond the Basics

One of the marvelous things about having a child is that it awakens your own creativity. Make this room a fun room. Nobody has to be serious. You can copy anything. In the eight-to-thirteen age group this room will become a laboratory for experimentation and self-expression.

1. *Paint bands of color,* filling the entire space between doors, to dazzle the eye. Use a small hand roller and make "waves" of color. After one color is completely dry, apply a new color to the unpainted area, allowing space for a third color. Supergraphic. Superfun.

2. *Make a patchwork rug.* Collect small samples of patterned and colorful rugs. On a large piece of brown paper lay out the design. Use two-sided Scotch tape to hold the pieces in place temporarily. Hunt around for the missing pieces until the design is pleasing. Move the shapes and pieces around to get the best layout. When you've gathered all your rug pieces and put them in place, measure rug size and buy a piece of burlap (for backing) the right size plus four inches all around. Buy two-sided heavy-duty carpet tape, and tape the pieces to the burlap. When all are secure, turn the hem in on the burlap to create a finished look. Buy a piece of thin nonskid rubber-loc liner and you have an easy, fun, and individual area rug.

3. *Create a private nook* where no one but the child is allowed to go. Install a curtain rod on the ceiling four feet from a corner to create a triangular nook. Make a pair of curtains using pleater tape and a bright fireproof material, using one-width 50-inch-wide fabric each side, or a pair of single sheets. This corner can be used to give shows, as a place to go and be alone, a place to nap, to dream . . . to be. Use grosgrain ribbon, attached to cup hooks, to tie back the curtains when this corner area needs light for reading or playing. Add a few pillows for sitting on the floor.

4. *Create an imaginative display wall* to house your child's growing collections, using some of the wooden blocks (left over from an earlier era) as brackets. At the lumber store, buy a variety of narrow shelves ranging from 4 to 8 inches deep and 12 to 24 inches long. Paint the brackets and shelves a potpourri of happy colors, depending on the collection, and nail the brackets to the wall with brads (nails with no heads). The movable shelf is more flexible. If you are displaying rocks and minerals, paint the shelf a rich green or chocolate brown or wine red. Shells might show up well against a midnight blue. Paint one side of the shelf a light color and the reverse side a dark color for variety.

5. *Stencil.* Buy a stencil kit and some lively colored latex semigloss paints at your local paint store. Paint flowers on the headboard, desk, or lamp shade. Create a chair rail with the child's name, interests, favorite song or TV star. All the numbers and letters are in the kit waiting to be put to use. Label a series of painted coffee tins on a window ledge for order: chalk, pencils, markers, jacks, marbles, clay, oragami, jewels, collage, coins. Paint on clear polyurethane to protect the sides from chipping.

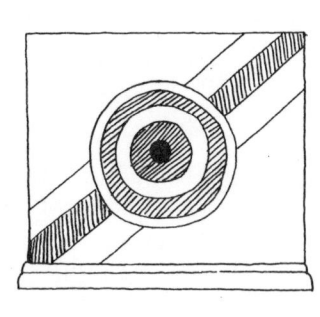

6. *Supergraphic.* Buy a supergraphic kit in a paint store that sells graphic diagrams, use a semigloss latex paint, and with your child, paint a graphic on the wall. If you don't want your child to paint directly on the wall, buy a special acrylic strippable paper which accepts paint very well, comes in a 108-square-foot roll, and can easily be removed or changed. There are good graphic decals available, but the paint kit makes it so easy and offers an infinite variety in color and form.

7. *Buy some strippable put-ons.* Select Walt Disney characters or zoo animals, frogs, elephants, giraffes, lions, birds, or butterflies, ranging from 12 inches small to 6 feet tall, and apply them to a door. A set of birds might go on the ceiling, an elephant over the bathtub. When you want to remove them, they strip off easily. Emalj paint is superior paint for this because it has an extra grind of pigment and has a smooth finish. Scotch tape and strippable put-ons should not hurt a plaster wall painted with Swedish Emalj oil paint; crisp white walls show off the design.

8. *Buy a Contempo white writing board;* write on it with dri-erase vivid-color markers, which can be easily erased. Your child will use this for remembring special dates, for homework, art

work, lists, and endless fun. They are metal framed; magnets will stick to the white surface. Contempo offers a wide range of sizes and they can be mounted, or used on an easel. This writing board can be used to announce plays and dramatic skits now, and twenty years later the same one might be used to make business presentations.

9. *Buy portable plastic storage system,* in a bright color, from Sam Flax. There are different models, all plastic, and you pick your own components. These mobile storage units have swing-out trays, are adjustable, and can be used as end tables, as a supply table, kitchen cart, sewing box, film-supply holder. Years from now they could be used in the bath to hold towels, supplies, and plants.

10. *A light box* may be invaluable for the child who shows artistic talent or an interest in graphic art or cartography. You can buy or make a portable box for viewing slides, for tracing maps and illustrations from books. A light box can also display a mineral or shell collection. When a drawing made with Magic Marker on thin white marker paper is mounted on the light box, the light box charges the picture with life.

11. *Make cutouts*—animals, dolls, a dollhouse, a puppet theater, or a miniature football field—out of white foam-core sheets, then decorate with Magic Markers. You can buy foam core in sheets as small as 22 by 28 inches and as big as 48 by 96 inches. These thin sheets of foam are easy to cut and decorate, and children in this age group can work with it, too.

12. *Buy a beach umbrella* (in a primary color or stripes) and use it in the corner of your child's room to create a gay, whimsical mood for a special place for the child to go to read and just be. The umbrella lowers the ceiling height and can be purchased at a furniture store where terrace furniture is sold. You can buy a heavy iron stand to securely rest the umbrella in place and when you are off to the beach, bring the umbrella!

Chapter 6

THE ADULT YEARS
(age thirteen on)

. . . All grown-ups were once children—
although few of them remember it. . . .

The Little Prince
ANTOINE DE SAINT-EXUPÉRY

There are few successful adults who were not
first successful children.

ALEXANDER CHASE
Quoted in Kansas City *Times*
Seen in *Reader's Digest*
January 1976

ADOLESCENCE

Adolescence can be a difficult age for parent and child to live through. While your boy or girl may not yet be a fully mature, fully developed adult, he or she is no longer a child. The adolescent begins to view himself in a new way and to revise some of his assumptions about himself in relation to family, friends, the world.

BOYS AND GIRLS ARE DIFFERENT

Up until now we've stressed the many similarities between environments for boys and girls, but in adolescence, when male-female identities tend to become increasingly important, there may be a stronger drive to have these differences reflected in the young person's room.

PARENTAL AND PEER INFLUENCE

Parental influence continues to be enormous in the teens, but, also, the adolescent wants especially to be accepted by his friends and to break away somewhat from the family—be more independent. (Margaret Mead points out in her book *Family of Man* that only recently have girls been allowed to become "persons" before they have become mothers.) The adolescent should be given more opportunities to make choices.

Of course, while many adolescents talk of freedom, individuality, this is also a stage of great conformity, for the most part, especially as regards peers.

BIG CHANGE IN ROOM ENVIRONMENT

When your child becomes an adolescent, her old room may be in for some real changes, to reflect a new awareness. Many clients have told me that for their adolescent child, a room of his or her own is a much needed retreat—a private place to go and read, have locks on things, hiding places, to be alone to figure things out in his own mysterious way. Clients tell me that for the first time they notice that their child automatically shuts the door to his room. Because it is becoming so necessary for the young adolescent to make his own plans and exercise certain levels of freedom, he may act as if he owned his own bedroom, as if the four walls are his.

THE ROOM BECOMES AN APARTMENT

This is the final stage at home when your child begins to make the transition toward having his own room at college, or a small studio apartment somewhere. He wants privacy. Why not let him fix up the room so that to some extent it functions as an apartment within the family context? There are many easy ways to make this subtle shift.

COLLECTING MATERIAL POSSESSIONS

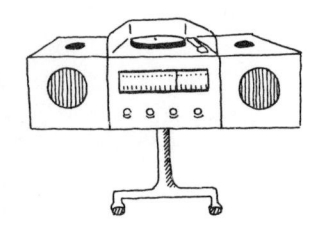

Now is the time when your child may really begin to collect possessions she will take away when she leaves home. Perhaps the old bed should be replaced with a mahogany poster bed, the table/desk with an antique desk. Now is when a child might like to acquire a few pieces of good furniture with the understanding that they are his whenever he leaves home. Some children have a great love for music, and a good set of stereo speakers and a turntable might replace the old phonograph. Being given a family piece of furniture at this age can be a wonderful thing because the child is old enough to know what he is most attached to and it gives him a feeling of continuity in a period when this can be significant.

CARED FOR

Anything you give a child at this age should be something she will take good care of. If you decide to invest in some possessions for your teen-ager, they'll have to be valued, respected and maintained.

TO CHANGE OR NOT TO CHANGE

Your daughter may be delighted to reflect her changed attitudes in her room decorations. She may suddenly want a very feminine traditional room, that is, an old-fashioned bedroom. (On the other hand, she may like everything just the way it is!)

THE QUESTION OF LABOR

If your teen-ager decides to redo his or her room, it's possible that he or she might make it a project with a friend. If you want to help and make it a joint project, all the better.

But whether you decide to make changes by buying new furnishings, or not, there are many inexpensive ways to convert a child's place into a place for the young adult and adult years.

WALLS

Because there is a strong drive toward being and expressing oneself, this is a good time to do some painting and get the room looking the way your child now wants it to look. Changing the walls to a new color, creating a new look, is an inexpensive and dramatic way to alter mood and atmosphere. And another wonderful thing about painting is that it forces you and your child to remove all the old pictures, Scotch tape, and banners from the walls, as preparation for a fresh start in wall hangings.

Wall Color Until now we've stressed the importance of opening up the space, in a child's place, through light walls, using panels of color in bright or contrasting colors, designs of color, or accents of color to stimulate. Now, when the adolescent probably uses the room more for reading and study, as a sitting room, dark walls might create a warmer and more cozy atmosphere. The boy who has lived with a red-white-and-blue theme might now prefer dark brown cork wallpaper for his walls. Or, the girl who has had white walls with multi-colored accents might still like white walls but prefer a more unified use of accents, in pink or cool blue. So much can and should be expressed through the use of color.

The son who picks a terra-cotta color for his walls should not be told by his mother that he always loved baby blue! Maybe he did, but he may not want to be reminded of it now. Dark colors do tend to close a room in and absorb light; however, much of the daylight hours are now spent, by the adolescent, at school or in other activities.

FLOORS

While a bare floor worked well for the young child, for the young adult, carpeting—a large overall rug—might give the room the added warmth welcomed at this time. The games played in this room now probably won't require the hard surface of a wood floor that was so useful when the child was younger.

Carpeting   Unless you are willing to put in wall-to-wall carpeting of good quality which will be appropriate in design, weave, and color years from now, I'd hold off on this expensive carpet solution. However, if your son or daughter plays a musical instrument—or a stereo—a shaggy carpeting, wall-to-wall might be a worthwhile investment, to help buffer the sound. If you decide on wall-to-wall, you might try buying carpet squares that come with a sticky back your child can easily lay himself. They are relatively inexpensive (dime stores carry carpet squares), and you can throw them out when the child leaves home.

A Rug Goes with the Child   If your child doesn't express a preference for wall-to-wall carpeting, a rug might be the most practical solution. Rugs can be sent out to be cleaned, rugs can be turned around to even out wear and dirt, and—a very important consideration—a rug can go off to college or to another room in the house and eventually to your child's first apartment. Few young people today can afford to buy a good rug with their beginning paychecks and they'd be grateful to have some of their own familiar things to start them on their way.

What Kind of Rug?   Your child can guide you about rug color and design, but it's hard to find a bargain when it comes to rugs. Design Research carries brightly colored two-sided Dhurrie rugs from India which are practical, inexpensive, and lively. Or, your son might be glad to have an old oriental rug. As everyone knows, oriental rugs wear endlessly and don't show dirt. Or, your child might prefer a bare floor, or one with bright area rugs.

Select a rug with a tightly woven pile so it will wear well and won't collect dirt. Many flatly woven rugs are two-sided which means you can turn them over when one side gets dirty. Flat woven rugs are easy to fold up, move, and store.

A smaller, better rug, one from Greece, India, Portugal, Spain, or Tunisia—in colors and a design your son or daughter really likes could be a present of lasting value and eventually could be used almost anywhere.

WINDOWS

Most children this age will want an opaque window shade to draw, regardless of other window treatments. Except for shutters, most window treatments can't be transported to a new location successfully, so I suggest keeping your window expenses to a minimum. If you plan eventually to use this room as a guest room or family sitting room and your teen-ager wants curtains, make a selection that is either inexpensive enough to be replaced easily when your child leaves home, or one that you will enjoy living with when this room switches roles.

Sheets at the Window Don't forget that sheets can be made into an easy and very inexpensive curtain treatment, to add color and pattern at the window. This is an idea many people have suggested, and it's a good one from the standpoint of value. If it doesn't matter that the curtains draw, you can simply hang up a pair of brackets on the top of the window trim and run the sheet heading through a rod. On a very wide window (six feet or more) use two sheets per width. To clean is as simple as changing the sheets on a bed.

Modern Venetian Blinds A simple practical solution at the window is the Riviera blind which has been mentioned earlier. They are one-inch-wide aluminum slats, come in a big selection of good clear colors, and offer complete light control. Transparent nylon cords replace the wide, old-fashioned venetian blind tapes, giving these blinds a modern, clean appearance.

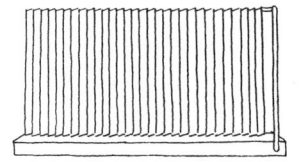

LIGHTING

The teen-ager is well aware of the psychological effects of different kinds of lighting. Some young people I've worked with have wanted their rooms to look like a dark den, with yellow and red lights. However, for reading, homework hobbies, and games, good lighting is required. There are so many modern designs in lamps and light fixtures available today at moderate prices; one of the first investments to make in this changed room are some good lamps. Also, if the lamps go on to college and after, this guarantees a long life.

Good Inexpensive Lamps   The most popular lamp is the architect's lamp, and smaller, inexpensive copies of this original design. Stationery stores and art supply stores carry good desk lamps; select a chrome or brass finish, which will go with everything. If you find a lamp you like in a battleship-gray enamel, brush on an enamel paint in a color you prefer. Tensor lights are handy for desk or on a piano for reading music because they focus light where it's needed. When selecting lamps for your soon-to-go-away-from-home child, be practical. How portable is the lamp? Many come apart for easy packing. Fragile lamp shades may look okay but may be too inflexible for a teen-ager. Flowered porcelain lamp bases might be more appropriate later, when your daughter has her first home.

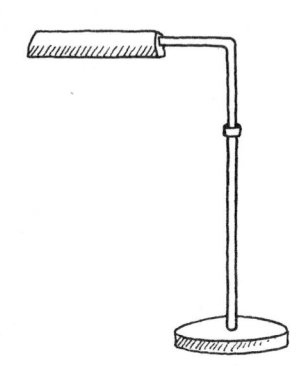

A Student Lamp   Buy a simple, brass-finished adjustable standing lamp with a brass shade. This "student lamp" is good near a bed, a card table, for a reading chair. Department stores are now selling them quite inexpensively.

Bed Light   By far the best reading light for the bed is a wall-mounted light. A lamp on the night table just isn't as flexible, and the lamplight may miss your child's book entirely.

The best wall lights have either a swing arm, or a gooseneck, or an adjustable can on a pivot. These features allow your child to adjust the direction in which the light falls.

Desk Light   If your son or daughter is an architect or artist he or she will want to have a clamp-on architect's light which extends and provides good light over a large surface. The lamp should be visible but not in the way. A small solid base is best so that it won't interrupt the flow of surface space. An arm or some sort of adjustability is always handy, particularly if this light also has to illuminate a nearby typing desk. Don't underestimate teen-agers today; they are very interested in function, when it comes to interior design.

MORE STORAGE

As many of the adolescent child's possessions as possible should be stored inside his own room, so more space for books, clothes, files may be needed. Most in-season sports equipment, especially if you live in an apartment, can be stored in the child's room and closet. Hang clamp hooks high up in a closet for skis, poles, tennis rackets, and baseball bats, as discussed in Chapter 5. Also, your child may now need more storage space for clothes, shoes, books, and papers.

FURNITURE

This room will now be set up in a more permanent way. Many teen-agers like their rooms to have daybeds and have the appearance of a sitting room. Games are still played but different kinds of games than in past years, requiring less rearrangement of furniture. Games now are played at a card table or desk.

Depending on the child, this room rearrangement could be quite an exciting project.

Furniture Requirements   The furniture changes need not be radical. If your child had twin beds before, they could now be used as daybeds, set at right angles. The desk gains in importance as does a comfortable swivel chair on casters at the desk. If there is room and there is an extra comfortable chair in the house, it could provide a nice place for reading. Your child might want a card table set up for games and projects or for typing, in order to keep the desk free and clear for work.

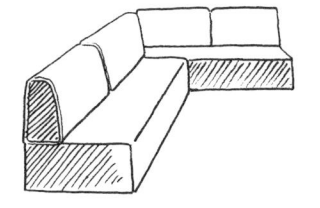

As long as there is a firm mattress for sleeping, a desk, chair, reading light, and storage space, there are no other specific requirements for this bedroom.

FABRICS

Claire had been sharing a bedroom with her older sister, who then went off to college. Everything in the room had seen a lot of wear and tear, and Claire's mother offered to pay for fabric to give the room an overhaul. Claire picked out the fabric from a display in a department store—a display of a canopy bed completely covered from top to bottom in a lily-of-the-valley sheet design. Ruffled bed canopy, ruffled pillow shams, a set of sheets, quilted coverlet, and ruffled flounce—the bed was a dream. Claire bought a set of these sheets and a quilted lily-of-the-valley coverlet, and within minutes, her bedroom was transferred into a May garden.

So far, not even sewing was required. Now there was only one thing missing: the canopy. One afternoon after school, Claire went to see the bed display again to study the canopy and try and figure out how to make one. Claire's father studied it too, and he agreed to make the canopy, using 2-by-2-inch boards and attaching the top frame to the bedposts. The posts were bolted to the wood frame of the bed.

Claire and her mother bought four more sheets and cut off eight inches from the bottom of each sheet for a gathered ruffled canopy which they put on the outside, unlined.

Bedspreads   Color comes first. Teen-agers, for the most part, want lots of color. The bed is still a place to flop on, sometimes with friends. Be sure the bedspread selected is machine washable. There are many strong solid-color blankets which can tuck into a bed frame and give a neat appearance. Plaid ones are nice, too, but tend to be more expensive. If you have a good-looking "car" blanket that isn't in use, ask your child if he would like this at the foot of his bed as an extra throw. There are many solid ribbed-cotton bedspreads and bed throws you can buy inexpensively, as well as a large selection of quilted sheets to use as bedspreads, most of them reversible.

COLOR

Teen-agers, like younger children, should be encouraged to express themselves through the use of color. The colors teen-agers pick on their own are often what sticks as "their" colors for years to come. The colors they dress in at this age are not always representative of the colors they have preference toward in their surroundings.

The room, their private place, becomes the true place for personal expression, and color is the way individuality is communicated most easily.

Color Test There is a book called *The Lüscher Color Test,* which outlines a way to reveal personality through color. I've found it interesting to use in my design work—and also in designing my own home. Color definitely expresses inner mood and psychological feelings, and the colors you like at one period may not be your favorites at another time. Maybe your teen-ager would benefit from taking the Lüscher test; the Lüscher book is available in paperback and it comes with colored cards to use for the test.

ACCESSORIES

All the things in a teen-ager's room should tell a story about the life and development of the child. By now, strong outside interests have developed, and the teen-ager is accumulating items of value. On the walls might be ribbons and medals won in athletic events. Trophies and awards are close at hand. In the room there might be a piano, a stereo or hi-fi set, a good am-fm radio, an alarm clock, a movie camera, a typewriter, a microscope, a set of reference books, a stamp collection, and a set of miniature soldiers. Another room could have posters of rock singers on all four walls, a bike hanging from hooks on the ceiling, in one corner a set of drums with a guitar, a record player and a cabinet filled with records.

What the teen-age child is interested in will show in this room. Model airplanes, travel posters, ballerinas, tennis players tell a story. If this room is given over to the child for the child's own use, it will grow into an interesting scrapbook of the child's travels, hobbies, friends, and the time in which he lives. The room will reflect a person in transition.

MAINTENANCE

Keeping things in order is a necessary discipline throughout life. If these adolescent years slip by and your son or daughter is allowed to develop untidy personal habits, chances are the future will be a continuation of this pattern. If this is his place, he should help maintain it, as in the past.

Setting Up a System   It should be possible to keep this room in order without its taking a lot of time. Your son or daughter might now take over completely, and set up a system of order and maintain it. It doesn't matter how it works as long as it can be kept up. Offer help in setting up the system, but try not to get into the habit of actually picking up after your adolescent.

TELEPHONE

This tends to be an age when young people develop telephonitis —one phone call after another. If the parent is not going to supervise the activity of the teen-ager while he is in his room, a telephone is a dangerous drainer of time—to say nothing of the expense. Automatically, when teen-agers are bored, they dial a friend to see what the action is. At least if the teen-ager has to get up and leave his room and go to a hall or the kitchen to telephone, that is a way of reminding the child to hurry it along. Giving a child his own phone is designed to free the telephone for parents, not to have the child call her classmates in place of buckling down to homework. I think an extra phone for a child's room is an unnecessary luxury.

TELEVISION

Through twelfth grade, I feel it wrong to have a television in a child's place. Recent statistics show that an average child this age spends more hours viewing television than going to school. There are wonderful things on television, both entertaining and educational, but I think viewing should be selective and shared.

THE COMPLETE OVERHAUL:
ONE EXAMPLE

If your teen-ager wants to create a completely new kind of room
—modern when his room has been traditional, for instance—and
if you can afford it, something wonderful could result. Your
child might be quite advanced in design knowledge and understanding. One young man I know got a vision, and his mother
went along with Michael's desire to change everything in his
room.

Michael built a plywood platform 10 inches high, put his
mattress on top, and then built two platform end tables the same
height as the bed (16 inches high including the mattress)—a
bed-and-end-table console, in the sky. Then he painted the room
lemon yellow—floor, ceiling, walls, bed platform, and end tables.
Michael loved to read in bed and so he hung two gooseneck wall
lights (also lemon yellow) over his platform bed. One of Michael's two closets was used for books and general storage. By
removing the door (and storing it away for future use), Michael
was able to build bookshelves in the closet, using standard strips
and brackets; also, he fit his chest of drawers into the closet, too.
Another bookcase had been Michael's when he was three; it
stored his blocks! Michael painted it yellow and added it to the
"new" room. The only other furniture in the room: a yellow
Parson's table, a yellow bentwood chair, and three filing cabinets
painted yellow (under the window ledge). On his Parson's table
is a yellow architect's light.

Michael's room wouldn't be for everybody, but he certainly
thrived in it. He loves plants and grew them at the window on
top of his files.

Beyond the Basics

1. *A personal wall hanging.* Buy a big 3-by-4-foot sheet of
Homasote at the lumberyard. Have your child paint it a bright
color, a color that will be a good background for photographs,
mementos, magazine and newspaper cutouts, posters, quotations,
pictures, letters, and invitations. With pushpins, let your child
tack different things onto the board and rearrange them until it's
pleasing. Cut out some pictures; leave others as is. When this is
finished, use rubber cement to glue down the arrangements and
then seal it with clear shellac. Tape the sides of the panel with

colored Mystic tape and attach horizontally to the wall with screw eyes and picture wire.

2. *Hang a collection* of quilts or small prayer rugs on the wall for decoration and sound absorption.

3. *Buy a pair of earphones* for your teen-ager to keep that rock music private.

4. *Make a shadow box* (a good idea for adding dimension and a useful display area). Make a two-inch-deep box (any size around) and have a piece of quarter-inch-thick glass made to fit the top. Have the lumberyard channel the frame to receive the glass so the glass slides in and out from the top. Your child can glue postcards or mementos to the inside back, or place inside a stamp collection, a shell collection, or pressed flowers. Hang the box on the wall or put it on a wall ledge. Add others in different sizes. Paint them in different colors.

5. *Make a storage rack for music.* A teen-ager may be just as interested in a music library as in a library for books. Build an 18-inch-deep shelf and support it on heavy-duty angle irons. Divide the space so there is record storage next to the turntable, a place for tapes and speakers. Above this shelf, hang a sheet of Homasote, covered with a piece of colorful felt, and supply a box of pushpins. Your teen-ager will soon fill this with music scores, pictures of rock stars, and musical memorabilia.

6. *Panel a wall* with 3-inch-wide pine beams installed vertically and spaced one inch apart. The paneling adds texture, warmth, and depth. The wall space between the panels should be painted a color that complements the natural panels. Bright yellow, orange, blue, or red would be high contrasts to the pine and extremely lively. If something more subdued is wanted, use earthtone colors, more neutral in hue and closer in color to the panels (beige, light brown, rust, putty, or luggage brown). This wall treatment can be executed just as successfully when the wall and the panels are painted the same color. White on white gives the feeling of a greenhouse when plants are hung from hooks. No matter what finish is used, the wall has a dimension not possible with a flat solid surface. (This is a great idea for hiding a rough wall surface in bad condition.)

Also, pushpins can be used in this soft pine, to hang posters, photographs, a calendar, and use screw hooks to hang some keys, a belt, plants, beads, ties, dog collar, or hats.

7. *Buy a Gro-Lux lamp for plants.*   The lamp is made by GTE Sylvania, and gives a perfect balance of red and blue light, the best for growing plants. You can also purchase a simple, good-looking fixture with an adjustable reflector for varying the light that makes plant-growing convenient. Or, just screw a special plant-grow light into an old gooseneck lamp and aim it at the plants on the window sill.

8. *Install ceiling-track lighting.*   Buy wall fixtures or flood can lights. Move them back and forth along the track where needed in the room.

Re-use this system when you move, and add new wall wash fixtures and track, to expand lighting if used in a larger room or when you need more light.

9. *Use colored glass* on top of floor up can lights to change mood and lighting effect when room becomes a sitting room.

10. *Hang batiks on the wall.*   To add color, texture, pattern, and warmth, hang inexpensive Indonesian batik cotton cloth on the walls. Hang with tiny nails (brads).

11. *Turn a bathroom into a darkroom.* Hang a no-light shade in the window for room darkening.

12. *Buy a strongbox with a set of keys.*   Keep a record of money earned and spent in a small accountant's notebook stored in the box. If you can't buy a box in anything but gray, spray it with three coats of enamel in a lively color that inspires you to save.

13. *Paint the doors with fluorescent paint.*   Each one a different color. Add a wall graphic in the same fluorescent colors.

14. *Store dumbbells under the bed* along with an exercise mat for morning exercise. Hang a chin bar in doorway. Caution: Have this done professionally to assure safety.

15. *Stretch flags on the walls.*   Sew on small plastic rings and attach with brads.

16. *Make a hollow-cube table* with a hinged side so all games can be stored carefully, and use the cube table as the game table. Paint the top for chess. Put a lip on edge for puzzles.

17. *Buy a map holder* to store maps of the world.

Chapter 7

WHEN THE CHILD LEAVES THE NEST

You can't go home again.

THOMAS WOLFE

WHOSE ROOM IS IT?

I've been in houses where parents have kept their child's room virtually the way it was left when the child went away to college ten years before. Certainly if parents don't need the space themselves, aren't moving, and therefore don't have to consolidate their accumulation of possessions (and their child enjoys returning to visit his parents and staying in "his" room), this is a good solution. For many, however, it isn't practical or realistic.

WHEN THE CHILD LEAVES HOME FOR COLLEGE

This is a natural breaking point. The child's place at home is no longer such a sacred domain, especially after the first year away. Many personal treasures, memorabilia, paraphernalia, and possessions are taken off to be used in the setting up of a college room. The room at home, half stripped, and with the child away, should be thought of in this new light. At what point can parents justify using this space personally?

The longer the child lives away from home on a regular basis, the less necessity there may be to keep this room a child's place. As long as you have a welcoming bed and an area where the child can unpack and get hold of his things, that may be enough. To try and maintain things as they were may not be what the child really wants because he has outgrown the "transparent walls" of childhood and is in the process of gradually leaving the nest.

CHANGE THE SPACE

Instead of letting this room go unused when the child is away, transform it into an extra room so that when the child isn't home on vacations, it can be a useful guest room, or studio, or sewing room, or family sitting room. One parent I know uses her grown daughter's room as a workroom for her committee work, using the surface space of her daughter's two single beds for all her papers.

Depending on the layout of your house or apartment and the size of the space and your family, you may feel this room should be converted to be used entirely for another purpose.

When the child goes off to work or college and then gets his own place, it's a giant step toward fulfillment as a person. When this happens, use this opportunity to adjust your available space toward your own personal goals and environmental improvements.

PART III

How to Divide a Child's Place: Sibling Privacy

Chapter 8

PARTITIONS AND DIVIDERS

. . . they do not even know how much
more is the half than the whole.

HESIOD

C. 700 B.C.

Less is more.

ANDREA DEL SARTO

This chapter and the following one deal with how to design one room to work for two or more children. Everyone has his own reasons for deciding to put children together in a room, and it can work successfully even for boys and girls in a span of ages if you plan for each child's specific needs and provide some islands of separation between each child.

WHY DOUBLE UP?

First, it might be useful to focus on why you are putting more than one child in a room. Were you an only child and always lonely? Or, more likely, are you running out of space? Do you feel it is a good thing for children to learn to live together and share? Are you going through a family crisis and find you want to tighten the space to provide a feeling of more security? Or, do you think it will be easier on you to have the children together in one space? Think first about your reasons, as they will affect the design you choose.

I know a father who was an only child, brought up in a big house; he rattled around on the third floor and loved being alone. (*His* father thought it was character-building to learn to be alone, separate.) When my friend became a father he then insisted on separate rooms for his own three children, even though his two boys begged to be allowed to have bunk beds together. He considered privacy a great priority; but he has produced children who are loners. They don't know how to join in at camp. They can't share or participate. They don't like team sports.

Privacy *is* important and being alone is essential, but there should be a balance. If your children have to share a room, it could be a real plus in their development, especially if you handle the environment creatively. Think about what you feel is important, and try to balance your design decisions so that whether your children share a room or not, they have exposure both to companions and sharing, and privacy.

SIBLING RIVALRY

If you do decide to put the children in the same room, one thing to keep in mind and plan around is sibling rivalry. It is perfectly normal, and I would guess your pediatrician will reassure you in this matter.

The older child is likely to feel some conflict at having to move over and share with someone he sometimes finds "babyish." How you handle the doubling-up is all important.

But there is no need to provide separate rooms for your children as long as you provide separate areas for privacy and special privileges within each space, especially, at first, for the older child.

Your attitude will make a lot of difference in whether your older child feels privileged or deprived.

KEY ELEMENTS IN A SHARED SPACE

Throughout this book we review the important elements that make up the space in a child's room and stress which ones are most important during the different stages of a child's growth. In a shared room, privacy becomes especially significant from the point of view of design; noise is another real factor. Space is at a premium, and providing adequate storage space is a major challenge. Because each child has a definite personality and needs to express that unique self in this child's place, the room cannot neglect these disparate characteristics or dissimilar qualities. In some cases, the only solution is to partition the room into two completely separate spaces. We'll explore various space possibilities, to help you determine what the best solution is for you and your children.

DIVIDING UP SPACE

Create emotional separations, as well as physical barriers, where possible. Each child wants to feel that he or she can have an individual place.

First, determine your approach by studying the restrictions of your available space and the different needs of each child based on age, sex, and personality. Your daughter, who brings homework from school, needs different things from your preschooler. Where can she study while her younger brother sleeps? Small children, as discussed earlier, need large quantities of space to play in, including floor space, while an older child needs a desk.

Think about what stage each of your children is in, the main activities each engages in, and plan a space for as many of the major ones as you can.

No matter what your current needs are, they too will change and shift as your child or children grow into new stages, with new needs. So a flexible arrangement, readily adjustable to changing conditions, is a good idea.

RULE OF THUMB ON DIVIDING A ROOM

One rule of thumb: It's not a good idea to divide a room if it means you have to make the room's length less than its ceiling height. For instance, if your room has a nine-foot-high ceiling, and you divide the room so one wall is seven feet long, it will create a cagelike feeling. To an adult, a large room with a high ceiling is ideal but that's not necessarily true for a small child. A child wants some boundaries and divisions to break the horizon. Actually, studies have indicated that children like large rooms they can break up into small areas, and they also like low ceilings. They will build stepping blocks high enough to be able to touch a ceiling.

If you find you have a small space, with a fairly high ceiling, develop the horizontal areas to lessen the exaggerated vertical feeling. For example, use steps that go up to a platform or loft which then leads to a bunk bed. Build a loft with a solid *high* plexiglass rail (for seeing out) which can be for sleeping or just a quiet place to be. Or block it in with sturdy wood spindles, arranged close together.

Before we discuss flexible partitioning of space, I want to talk briefly about permanent dividers.

PERMANENT DIVIDERS FOR A ROOM

I know couples who build expensive additions on their homes because "the children have outgrown their quarters." One family had their baby in a little sewing room, but this little girl got big so quickly that a whole new wing was added to the house. Now this girl is married, lives far away, and these added rooms are empty. I worked for this family and know the space in the house well. There was a large square room that could have been shared with her brother, thereby saving the expense of building an addition to the house.

Of course, if you live in an apartment, you can't add on; you have to find a way of using your available space. Today, with space such a precious commodity, few of us can waste an inch.

Building a "Permanent" Partition If you feel you need a true wall division, you can build a plasterboard or sheet-rock partition (partial length or full) as low or as high as you wish. This rather permanent wall division should be positioned thoughtfully, especially so that the light and air from your window or windows can feed both "rooms." Air circulation is important and most solid dividers take away air unless you retain a window in each divided space. If this is impossible the way your space is laid out, don't have your partition go all the way up; in this way you can create a wall and still have light and air.

When you plan a partition for a room, do a floor plan in scale so you visually understand how your space will look when it's diminished. Note heat sources, electrical outlets, and closet locations. Try to arrange your partition in such a way that each room has its own door even if this means more partitioning.

For example, you might have a rectangular room with only one doorway. If you were to put up only one partition separating the space into two equal-size areas, "A" child would have to walk through "B" child's space to get to his or her own room. However, if you make a narrow hallway, approximately 26 to 30 inches wide (depending on how much space you can borrow) and long enough to enclose "A" child's space, you are creating an entrance hall to "B" child's room, providing two private areas with a door that can be closed. A room without a separate entrance is not a room!

ACOUSTICAL CEILINGS

There are tiles you can buy and install yourself that will help absorb sound, either in a permanently divided space or a temporarily divided space. While you are considering partitioning, also evaluate whether you should put in an acoustical ceiling. If you do, do not use asbestos because its flaking may be injurious to health. Heavy curtains at the windows will absorb some sound in a room, but possibly not enough

BUILDING MATERIALS

You can build, or have someone build, a partition out of wood and sheet rock. Use wood for a frame and sheet rock for the walls. The frame of the partition can be laid out on the floor of the divided area with wood strips nailed into place.

INSULATING A PARTITION

If you have a heat source in each part of the divided space, you may not require insulation. However, insulation need not be very expensive and can be easily stapled onto the wood frame, as a sound-absorption aid. For instance, Owens Corning insulation is available by the roll, and it can be applied to the wood frame with a staple gun.

PARTIAL SHEET-ROCK PARTITIONS

If the sheet-rock partition isn't going to be carried to the ceiling, frame in your area the same way you would if you were using a full partition, after determining how much space is to be exposed at the top.

ARTIFICIAL LIGHTS FOR A PARTITIONED WALL

If you need to have an electrician put in wiring or an extra outlet in your partition, you might want to add strips of daylight fluorescent lights at the top of the partially partitioned wall—creating a "wash" of light. On dark days this extra light might be a source of cheer. These fixtures come in stock sizes (the kind

you've seen under kitchen cabinets that light the counter top)
and are inexpensive to buy, install, and use.

WINDOW TREATMENT FOR PARTITIONED SPACE

If you are dividing a room with a floor-to-ceiling partition, another important factor for a child's place is natural light. Every
consideration should be made to bring in as much natural light
from the window as possible. If your child ends up with one window, you should play up the window to make it more important.

CEILING LIGHT IN HALLWAY

If by dividing a room you have a newly created hallway, you
might install a strong down can light, with a separate switch. If
you have an extra-long hallway, you may need two ceiling
fixtures.

DECORATING THE HALLWAY

If you create a separate hallway, you could add a wonderful
graphic on one wall, or paint the doors into the two bedroom
areas a bright primary color. If you plan to have painted floors in
the new bedrooms, you might paint this hall floor area a contrasting color. Chances are this hallway will be small and it could be
given some character if painted in an imaginative way. For example, in the hall you could print the child's first name or initials
in big block letters, vertically, on his door.

LOCATION OF CLOSETS WHEN PARTITIONING SPACE

If you have two closets in the room, ideally your partition will divide the closets so one will be in each child's new space. How-

ever, you may have a situation that forces you to give one child's place both closets, leaving the other space with none. In this situation, you might partition further to create a hall for the two children to share, each having a closet. One couple with twins had this problem to solve. Both closets were at one end of the room, so they created a bedroom hall closet area with a partial partition the same height as the top of the closets. For twins who have no seniority privileges, this seemed the fairest solution.

BUILDING A NEW CLOSET

If the space you are about to divide has only one closet, you may decide to partition the room and build a new closet for one child. After your space is laid out in scale on paper, you can determine where the new closet should be built. You might find you can put it in one corner which could give an otherwise ordinary space some added charm. Or, you may decide to take one entire wall and build floor-to-ceiling storage with a closet, drawers, a desk area, and high storage for off-season toys, equipment, and luggage.

CLOSET DOORS IN PARTITIONED ROOMS

When you are partitioning a room, you may find the standard closet door is too wide for your new, smaller space. The easiest thing to do is take the door off its hinges and replace it with two solid panels; one panel hinges on the left, one panel hinges on the right. Wooden louvered half-door panels also come in many stock sizes and you may find your lumberyard has some in the right size to fit your door. If your closet is in a corner and any kind of door would bang into a piece of furniture, I suggest hanging a pair of simple, washable curtains on a traverse rod. This curtain might match the sheets (or be a sheet) and/or curtains and be an attractive addition. Sometimes a laminated cotton material, like Marimekko, is a perfect solution for the small room closet door.

WOVEN-WOOD VERTICAL BLINDS FOR YOUR CLOSET

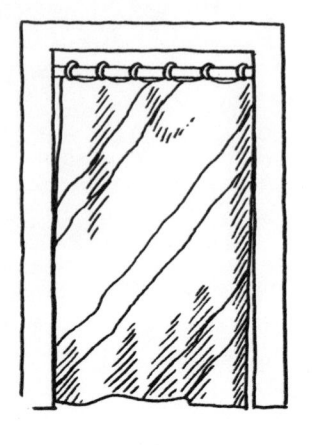

Another great space saver to replace the closet door is a vertically installed woven-wood blind. This can draw to one side, or draw from the center to each side.

CLOSET LIGHTS

Whenever possible, install a closet light for a child. Closets get stuffed with clothes and toys, and a good, strong light can be an incentive to keep it neat. Children have trouble remembering to turn their closet light out, however. Consider having the light triggered to go out when the closet door is closed. This way, the child is taught always to close the closet door. If you decide it's too expensive to install a light in the closet, be sure there is a strong ceiling light nearby.

LESS PERMANENT PARTIAL PARTITIONS

Study some of the partitions you see in offices, hospitals, and banks. Office designs are straightforward and created to be functional, and a great deal of research has gone into the results.

For example, Herman Miller has partitions called "Action Office Panels." There is no reason these office panels can't come right into your child's place.

A file bin could be used as a toy box. A display shelf could hold an ABC book. A tackable acoustical wall can be used for displaying posters and things of special interest. You can buy these panels in twenty-one colors, solid or in combinations. You can replace inserts in these panels—there are dozens of colorful graphics designed by the famous architect Alexander Girard which were made for this system. Alexander Girard selected the colors for the system as well, so they are alive clear colors, just right for your child's place. This system was designed so you can easily change things. Your ability to have whatever height you want from one inch on up means this system can be useful from the beginning and can travel to college dorm or home office in later years. Today's toy bins can be tomorrow's file bins; the low surface will eventually be raised to become a work surface. You can add panels to the ones you have because the panels have a track in them which allows you to buy and hang a variety of components. You can add shelves, Flipper doors (to hide clutter), more files or bins or display shelves. They are freestanding and are supported by the arrangement and combination of end panels. Even if you don't put two children in one room, you might want to consider something like this for a child who needs a confined area to study, away from the more playful elements in the larger part of the room. Think what possibilities this has for design, color, bulletin board, chalkboard, felt board, and anything you and your child's inventive mind can dream up.

One mother got so excited about her son's tackable acoustical wall divider that she bought one and put it in her studio so she could use it for squares of material she sews together and quilts and sells for profit!

TEMPORARY INEXPENSIVE DIVIDERS YOU MAKE YOURSELF

A 4-by-8-foot sheet of plywood on a wooden stand can be a movable divider, to create interest and walls within a space for your child—as well as privacy. You may get some ideas from magazine and catalogue pictures of designs you can build yourself, but take pictures with you to the lumberyard so you can get advice on stock materials you can use. And take measurements of the room, also, so you can try out different possibilities (using stock sizes), thereby saving labor and money.

CEILING-TRACK WOVEN BLINDS

Another way to solve the room-sharing-and-dividing problem is by having a ceiling track installed which holds a ceiling-to-floor, sliding woven-wood blind. The special plus about this kind of divider is that even an 18-foot wall can be instantly opened up, or closed off—quick and easy division. Also, the accordion woven-wood blind could be stacked—when not in use—out of the way in a narrow 11-inch stack, skinnier than half an average door width. A great space-saving and space-expanding idea.

As I mentioned, some rooms need to be divided, so you create a hall or walkway (to avoid disturbing a sleeping child), to allow access into another room. For example, you may have a master bedroom in your house or apartment which has a sitting room off it; and you are now using the master bedroom for the nursery and the smaller sitting room as a master bedroom. If the only way to get to the smaller room is through the newly created nursery, you could install a flexible divider so that you can get into your room, without having to go through the nursery. When this space is needed for the child's playtime, you simply push the woven-wood blind off to one side, out of the way.

A folding screen on a ceiling track is another excellent solution. Folding screens come in wood finishes and also in white painted wood panels, which add a lighter feeling to the space. They can be hung on a track which curves, too; the space doesn't have to be divided absolutely into two straight spaces. These can be especially effective for creating a room for an infant.

Avoid solid track dividers for your child's room because they block out light and air.

CEILING-TRACK CURTAIN

An even less expensive solution is to hang a ceiling curtain track and make a draw curtain out of sheets. Or, make the curtain out of felt for greater sound absorption. Sew on some contrasting felt shapes to add color and design. However, cloth isn't as sturdy, and children are likely to pull at the curtains in play. But the curtain effect would be an excellent idea as a divider to create an infant's room. And, you could make the curtain high off the floor, (easier for cleaning purposes), to divide just the visual space. You could buy shower curtains or make your own, with grommets on top for the hooks.

FLOOR TRACKS

Surface-mounted floor tracks can be dangerous because your child might trip and fall on the raised area of the track. A raised floor track gets in the way, also, when furniture is being moved around the room, and it limits how much floor space can be used for play. Eliminate this unnecessary barrier by either recessing the floor track or installing a ceiling track instead.

SLIDING PANELS ON CEILING TRACK

Sliding panels hung from a ceiling track are a flexible, safe solution to dividing space and can also become a color accent. The basic concept is simple, as you have a series of panels on separate tracks in the ceiling which extend down to the floor. They can slide across the room to completely separate the two areas, or to partially divide the space, depending on your specific need. For example, if you have a ten-foot wall to divide and you want always to have a panel of color and design separating each child's sleeping space, this panel could remain stationary while the others are on a track and slide across the room as required. You've seen a similar method of walls in panels in hotel ballrooms or corporation board rooms where a wall, when all the panels are closed, looks solid—when in fact, the wall panels can slide into the walls. The only difference here is you have one section, one panel, fixed, and the other panels slide and can stack next to this fixed panel—and across the room to divide space.

I've used this method often and always successfully. In North Carolina I worked on a house that was right on the water, with a wonderful view of the harbor. The kitchen, however, was walled off from this view completely. We removed the kitchen wall completely and replaced the solid plaster wall with five four-foot-wide wood panels. The five panels usually stacked to one side allowing 16 inches of uninterrupted view of the water. The one four-inch-wide stationary panel acted as a small wall for the living room. The entire kitchen was redesigned and became a living-kitchen. On social occasions, when there were large groups of people, these panels could slide across the entire area, hiding the kitchen from view.

Panels like these could separate the two beds in your children's room.

MATERIALS USED FOR SLIDING PANELS

Wood is used most often for these panels, but fabric can also be successful. I've hung a series of quilts on panels, and it has worked beautifully. This is not the solution for small boys who will tug at the quilts, however. You could stretch two different fabrics back to back inside a wood frame, which would act as a good sound absorber as well as providing color and texture.

If you want to use a cotton print for the panels, I recommend having it heavy-duty laminated so it will be more substantial and finger marks won't show.

LOW ROOM DIVIDERS

There are several low room dividers available for young children, which are reasonable in cost and have versatile functional possibilities. For example, you can buy a clothes locker designed for preschool children; its design encourages self-help by having clothes hooks at a child's level. Many units are on casters so they can easily be moved anywhere in the room. Use two at right angles and you've created a private corner.

Also available are straight low room dividers. One is a solid panel of hardwood in a natural finish, 48 inches wide by 33 inches high, with wide leg supports. This can be used as a display area while providing seclusion. It can also be covered with lively fabric or felt. This divider can easily be moved aside when all the space is required for play.

Another idea for a straight low divider is pegboard panels; they come with removable feet so you can make it vertical or horizontal—or, eventually, hang it on the wall.

DIVIDE WITH BOOKS

One of the most practical and colorful room-dividing ideas is to use bookcases. They can be purchased inexpensively unpainted, and you can paint them to match the room decoration. If you have four bookcase units, of similar size, have the book side of two face onto "A" child's side of the room and have two face onto "B" child's side. You might alternate front, back, front, back. Onto the back of each bookcase you might glue a poster, or tape up a child's painting, or cover it with a colorful fabric panel. This way, each child gets two sections of books and storage as well as two panels of wall space for hanging colorful things.

ROOM DIVIDERS THAT STORE THINGS

For a low wall divider that stores things, you might prefer to make an open cabinet on casters with shelves that hold plastic bins—a place for everything and everything in its place. Should your children outgrow this unit, you could use it yourself for storing sewing equipment, wrapping supplies, party favors, Christmas decorations, tools, candles, plant and potting supplies, household cleaners, etc. These plastic bins can be purchased in any houseware or hardware store and come in several different colors. For children sharing this divided space, buy half of the bins one color (for instance, red) and half of the bins white. Each child can get at his or her color bins from both sides of this dividing cabinet.

Another good storage idea that also divides space for a young child is two bookcase and storage units which can hinge together. You can use these units open at right angles, or close and lock them for the child's safety. I've used two of these hinged units in a room where two small children shared a room, and by giving each child his own storage cabinet, you also provide each child with the option of using the hinged cabinet as a room divider.

Other storage cabinets are available; look for one that is practical and well constructed. Unpainted-furniture stores often have a fine selection of cabinets that you can finish yourself. Many unpainted-furniture stores will paint the furniture for you for an additional charge of approximately 10 per cent.

HIGH STORAGE DIVIDERS

When your children are older, you may decide to use a substantially higher storage wall divider. These can be placed against the wall initially and later moved into the center of the room, providing double-storage access, shared by each child. By using a tall storage room divider you may find you have emotionally divided the space sufficiently so that you don't have to extend the unit the entire width of the room you are dividing. For example, on a 16-foot-wide space you may find an 8-foot unit, placed in the center of the space, would be separation enough. This placement of the storage unit will provide four feet of walk space on either side and will allow light, air, and heat to circulate freely between the two spaces.

BACK-TO-BACK HIGH STORAGE DIVIDER

Suppose you want to separate your two sons who are sharing a room, but you also want them to have one basic room. The boys are both old enough to need desk space, storage space, and privacy.

You could divide their room with a set of high storage units which sit back to back in the center of the room. This way, each child has his own storage unit and is separated from his brother by the thickness of the width of the two units. You can buy separate components and create a system.

LOCATING THE DESKS

Even though each child is on a different side of this tall dividing unit, and you have a solid wall further separating them over the desk area, I suggest taking additional precautions to provide privacy. This can be done by placing each child's desk at the farthest possible distance from the other. Place one desk at the far end of side A, and the other desk at the opposite end of side B. This would eliminate the possibility of the two boys playing tapping games or creating noise distractions.

HALF THE DIVIDER ON EACH SIDE

You may not need to buy two entire storage units and place them back to back. You may find you can use one high unit, facing "A" child's space, and one high unit right next to it, facing "B" child's space. The back of a unit becomes a solid wall to the other side, a place to hang a picture or Masonite for a bulletin board.

SELECTING HIGH STORAGE UNITS

Storage units come in various designs and vary in concept, function, quality, and price. You should pick a storage system you can add to, as you need more storage space. The more variable pieces in the unit there are, the better off you are because you can add slowly and then rearrange. Don't compromise on an enormous system which has flimsy shelf brackets or badly constructed drawers or hardware that isn't attractive. Some units have desks that drop down on a hinge and even beds that are contained vertically behind a door. This might be a solution to the space problem when two or more children are sharing one room; it gets the beds off the floor and out of the way, when they're not in use. Some of these units also have tables that unfold from behind a closed door so that when the table is not in use, it doesn't take up any space. Folding chairs can be contained inside this storage unit, too.

Look into all the partition possibilities before you make your choice, and remember, a unit that doesn't seem very sturdy in the showroom will surely fall apart when you get it home. So be sure the construction is strong.

The plus side of a wall storage unit is that the component parts can be moved easily if you relocate; also, they can be stored with clothes, books, desks, supplies, and clutter in one clean organized system. And they divide space in two as well. When dividing space for older children, the unit you select might be a storage system your child uses for years to come, in many different locations and rooms. Many of these storage systems can be knocked down to make moving and storage less difficult and expensive.

Chapter 9

OTHER WAYS
TO DIVIDE
A CHILD'S PLACE

We're too unseparate.
And going home
From company means
Coming to our senses.

ROBERT FROST
Build Soil—
A Political Pastoral

Once you've chosen your partition, you can go on to plan the other elements in a divided room's design.

HOW TO TREAT BEDS IN A SHARED ROOM

In Chapter 3, I discussed different kinds of beds to consider for a child's place. When two or more children share a room, space becomes limited, and beds require a big chunk of whatever space there is. Single beds used against one wall as bunk beds can work out well in many shared sleeping situations. The oldest child can use the top bunk until he or she no longer gets a kick out of the climb. Then they can switch. When the two children are older, and no one wants to be on top, use the beds as daybeds in a corner at right angles—by day as sofas, at night for sleeping. All you need is some big pillows or bolsters for the back, to decrease the depth and make them comfortable for sitting.

If you have two children, one boy, one girl, whom you want at opposite ends of the room, you might consider one of these bunk-bed-desk-storage units. This way one child can be fairly self-contained in one specific area and can have a free bed surface for creative play and overnight friends.

If you have a pair of single beds, each with one matching headboard, place the pair of beds at right angles in a corner so the headboards are reversed now and are on the foot of the bed. Have two daybeds with bolsters and corner pillows. For young children, this corner can house all their stuffed animals and girl's dolls. Or, separate the beds with a 30-inch-cube table between the two beds in the corner. Have the table be the height of the top of the bed mattress.

STORAGE UNDER BED

When two or more children share one room, you not only have the children who live there, you also have their friends. Even sleeping bags require floor space. A trundle bed, hidden out of sight under a bed, brought out only when needed, is an excellent idea for a shared room. If your room is set up in such a way that you don't have floor space for a trundle bed, be certain you use the space under the bed for useful storage. You can buy campaign beds which have drawers built right into the frame, or you can separately buy drawers on casters that slide under your bed. (Under-the-bed space is only a dust collector and a waste if you don't use it for necessary storage.)

LOFTS

You may find that the room you want to divide is so small that if you were to cut the room up in two slices, you'd have two very small spaces. However, your ceiling may be high and you don't want to waste that space. In this type of situation, a loft bed which you go up to on a ladder may be the answer. This idea is especially popular with older boys and energetic girls. By adding the upper and lower dimension, it gives the illusion of space where there is little and can add an extra sense of privacy to the sleeping alcove. Be sure the light in the loft area is on a separate switch and *in* the loft area so the child doesn't have to climb down the ladder to turn the light off, or climb down the ladder in the dark to turn the light on. Children love these lofts and they become indoor playgrounds when friends come over. Children need to roughhouse and play in their own environment, especially when bad weather sets in. Some of these play-sleep lofts hold five or six children, which is a great deal of fun for slumber parties.

POSITIONING OF BEDS FOR A SHARED ROOM

Beds coming out from the wall look like a guest room and break up too much valuable floor space. Consider placing your beds parallel to the wall, or in a corner at right angles. When you have a floating partial partition, you can place one bed on each side, parallel to the partition. This way each child has privacy, and one could read late at night and not disturb the other.

LIGHTING IN SHARED SPACE

Lighting here is terribly important. Each child needs certain individual lights, but there also will be certain lights that must be shared, so plan the lighting carefully.

Two lighting possibilities work especially well in a shared space—track lighting and swing-arm wall-mounted lamps. With a ceiling track you can add movable can lights which focus down on specific work-play areas. In addition to a ceiling span of lights, swing-arm wall lights are good near the bed and desk area. By using this arrangement, furniture can be rearranged freely without worrying about having to move lamps. You will also be saving precious space.

DESKS FOR SHARED ROOMS

If you are buying or making a desk, inquire at your local library about a desk with front, top, and side panels, called "carrols." Like a horse with blinders, the desk becomes an instant "think center" where a child can sit and concentrate. Two of these, placed far apart, could prove to be good aids when one child needs to study and the other does not.

FLOOR TREATMENT FOR A SHARED ROOM

Rugs in a shared room can become territorial dividers. A wooden floor, stained and polyurethaned or painted a color and sealed with several coats of polyurethane, with some small area rugs of Haitian cotton stripe or patterned Dhurries from India, could be attractive and provide a feeling of individual boundaries for each child as well. Or, you might find two rugs in different colors in the same design, or two in the same colors but different designs so that they relate but don't match.

If you have two children sharing a room, there is no need to go to the expense of wall-to-wall carpeting as insulation against noise unless you really want to.

DIVIDING SPACE BY COLOR

Let each child select his or her own color, as much as you can. Color is a wonderful way to divide your children's space and possessions. In a recent study the colors found to be most beneficial to a child's development were yellow, yellow-green, orange, and light blue. Red was well-liked by children but can have the effect of stirring aggressions; boys tend to like red even more than their second favorite choice, blue.

Let me mention again here that I recommend large doses of white for a child's place. Again, if you are painting the room at the same time you're dividing it, I think the best white paint on the market for a child's place is the Swedish enamel paint Emalj which comes in four finishes from matt to high gloss. It won't' yellow, is scrubbable, and will not be hurt by Scotch tape. The main reason for white is to lighten and brighten and liven the room and, most important, it will give a background for the spot color you want to add and change. The colors you use to create a scheme will actually help your child be more alert and receptive.

One room shared by two children whom I know had the ceiling, walls, and floor all painted yellow on "A" child's side and white on "B" child's side. Then, to add spice, the furniture was selected so that the section with the white walls got blue furniture, and the section with yellow walls got white furniture. Through the use of color the two areas projected entirely different moods.

The best colors in children's plastic storage bins are shades of red, orange, yellow, blue, black, brown, and white. Green, I have found, has a wider range of shades, but many are murky and drab. Be wary of the quality and clarity of color shades.

If the colors the two children choose clash, each child might be encouraged to choose his next favorite color. Let it be a game. The next favorite colors can be used boldly in the room as accents. Use white for shared items, like clothes hampers, wastebaskets, etc. If each child has a separate bin for soiled clothes, use one of their colored plastic bins. This way, the laundry can be done separately and returned in the same bin, which saves time sorting out the siblings' clothes.

Color and Closets   Paint "A" child's closet door red and "B" child's closet door blue. If there is one closet to share, draw a dividing stripe of each color. Or, if you have a good strong light in the closet, paint each half "their" color. Our daughters share a large closet, and I was able to hang double clothes racks so each child's clothes are separate; and, each child has six colored plastic "sky" hooks and several plastic storage bins in her color. This individual storage of personal items is important to your child. No matter how many sisters or brothers there are, no child likes being just one of the bunch. And, it is difficult to expect "A" child to pick up or be terribly responsible about "B" child's things. A color-code system can help siblings learn to share.

OTHER PERSONALIZED TOUCHES

You also might add a child's initials to his headboard, or monogram a girl's doll's sweater and bed coverlet. Or if your children have separate closets, you might put their names on their closet doors. Put name tags on personal clothing, favorite dolls, stuffed animals. Children love their own names and initials. Even a "C" cup for Chris and a "B" cup for Bonnie in the bathroom is a good idea.

Color-coded Drawers   If you have one large storage unit that is to be shared, designate which drawers are for which child and color code the drawers. This can be a fun game, and it's also practical for parents because it saves time in sorting out belongings. If you want to keep the drawers the same color, paint a thin stripe on each drawer. Or install hardware in the child's color, or hand paint on their initials, or write out their first names.

THE POSSESSIONS OF OTHERS

Children must develop respect for each other's treasures and property. Children who share rooms have to learn to ask—or "hands off." Even a small pink plastic torso from a broken-down doll can be important to the owner. In school, children share group property; the crayons go back in a communal crayon can. At home, your child should be able to advance to more expensive coloring pencils in order to create more subtle-colored drawings —as long as the pencils are cared for. Parents and teachers can't govern the rules of play children work out among themselves

when they are alone, but they can encourage and teach, through specific examples, a certain expected standard of behavior each child should try to learn; and they can provide a private place for each child.

A CHILD'S "SPECIAL CORNER" IN A SHARED ROOM

A snuggly corner can be a special place in a child's room. You might create a cozy reading and resting area by covering mattresses and using soft pillows, lowering the ceiling height through the use of bright colors or through simple dry-wall construction. Don't just drop a ceiling height for the purpose of creating a snug sheltered area; use the top area for storage or a fun house. Or, buy a bunk bed and don't put in the lower bed! You have created a playhouse.

The three children in a family that lived in a large Georgian house in Pitsburg, Ohio, found their favorite place to go—a huge walk-in closet with high storage shelves. They climbed to the top on a sturdy wooden ladder. This closet was so popular that the parents gave in, and it was used as the children's "tree" house for years! There were pillows and a thin rubber pad and blanket; the length of the closet had an outdoor scene painted by the three children—a perfect place to hide and be alone.

In the corner of your child's room you might build a big three-sided cube; and use the top for trains or model planes and the inside for your child's fun house, with a small rug, pillows, and playthings.

I was called into a lovely family's home to help organize the space in the children's room, which was shared by twin sisters. After we determined how to arrange shelves for necessities in their walk-in closet, we sat down with their mother to discuss colors. Mrs. Parker said she would like to make some bedcovers and curtains for the girls and wanted to discuss the colors with me. She wanted my ideas on the design and the materials. After a lively conversation, charged with color, we settled on doing patchwork gingham spreads of pink, pale green, yellow, pale blue, and soft orange. The curtains (which were to be cafe type) were to have panels in each of the alternating colors of the quilts. The girls individualized their spreads (they both wanted all the gingham colors) by each one designing her own quilt. Mrs.

Parker followed their patterns. These seven-year-old girls were busy drawing designs, indicating which colors went where, by using colored Magic Markers, creating different-colored shapes and patterns. Mrs. Parker followed each form and curve faithfully, and the results are glorious. Even when a wet book left an ugly, colored stain on one quilt, the girls' mother didn't get upset; she just patched over the soiled place.

The Parker twins wanted their space to be treated alike. Not all children who share a room agree.

I think it can be equally charming if the space is divided symmetrically, creating two separate feelings by using two individual color schemes and fabric groups. You probably do this often yourself when you have a large group for a dinner party and your tablecloths and china, silver, and glassware don't stretch far enough to match for the number of guests. Aim at finding what is the most pleasant and functional world for each child. Emphasize the things most enriching to each child; this is more important than having a perfectly co-ordinated scheme, especially when there are several chidren. A poster bed for an eight-year-old girl might be a treat, and, in the same room, her three-year-old sister might still find delight in her lower-to-the-ground world of a mattress on a wood frame.

Beyond the Basics

1. *Needlework a small rug* to put in front of each child's bed. Have each rug tell a special story. Include the child's favorite colors, flowers, animals, and add initials, a rhyme, or a poem.

2. *Build a multilevel platform* so the space is divided into territories without having a solid high barrier. One child's floor space would remain unchanged and the other child's space would be raised.

3. *Use wicker planters as room dividers.* Buy two (or more) wicker planters and locate them side by side so they divide the space. The older child might fill the planter with plants, while the younger child would have sand inside the metal liner like a stand-up sandbox. The planters could hold books or dolls or stuffed animals. These planters can easily be moved aside when a group of friends comes to play.

4. *Paint a rainbow* on one wall in a shared room. Have each child select six favorite colors and at the middle of the rainbow

pencil in a vertical dividing line. Each child will put his own colors in his half of the rainbow. If one child is too young, parents might help with the painting. Buy small tubes of acrylic paint and striping brushes which are angled to help keep the rainbow lines straight.

5. *Use mirror to create a window where there is none.* In a partitioned space when one child's area is without a window, hang large sheets of mirror on two adjacent walls so the child "feels" the benefits of the windows.

6. *Hang corner shelves* made of plywood beginning above the baseboard and going up the entire corner wall to approximately six feet high. Decide how big they should be depending on your space. Space each shelf 12 inches apart. Paint the shelves the wall color. These make wonderful, safe display areas. The older child gets the higher shelves. Paint the front edge of the shelf the color each child selects to keep them separated.

7. *Make a window* in your room divider. Cut out a window 24 inches wide by 36 inches high (have the window begin 28 inches from the floor). On both sides of the divider hang some tied-back short curtains so each child can close this opening easily. When the children want to play post office with friends or have a puppet show, they can use the "window" for their game. And when they want privacy, they can close the curtain.

I love you for what you are,
but I love you yet more
for what you are going to be.

You are going forward toward something
great. I am on the way with you and
therefore I love you.

CARL SANDBURG
I Love You

. . . Practically all environmental impacts
leave an imprint on the body and the mind.
This imprint is likely to be almost
irreversible, especially if it occurs early
in life. . . .

RENÉ DUBOS
Beast or Angel?
Choices That Make Us Human

SOME BOOKS I'VE ENJOYED READING

ALBERS, JOSEF. *Interaction of Color* Yale University Press, 1972

BENDICK, JEANNE. *The Human Senses* Watts, 1968

BEECHER, MARGUERITE, and BEECHER, WILLARD. *Parents on the Run* Julian, 1955

BERMONT, HUBERT. *The Child* Trident, 1965

BETTELHEIM, BRUNO. *Children of the Dream* Avon, 1970

———— *Love Is Not Enough* Avon, 1971

BIRREN, FABER. *Color in Your World* Collier, 1971

BREARLEY, MOLLY, and HITCHFIELD, ELIZABETH. *A Guide to Reading Piaget* Schocken, 1966

CAPLAN, FRANK, and CAPLAN, THERESA. *The Power of Play* Doubleday, 1973

CHABON, IRWIN. *Awake and Aware* Dell, 1969

CHURCHILL, ANGIOLA R. *Art for Preadolescents* McGraw-Hill, 1971

COHEN, DOROTHY. *The Learning Child* Vintage, 1973

DATTNER, RICHARD. *Design for Play* MIT Press, 1969

FRAIBERG, SELMA H. *The Magic Years* Scribner's, 1965

FROMME, ALLAN. *The ABC of Child Care* Simon and Schuster, 1956

GATTEGNO, CALEB. *What We Owe Children* Avon, 1971

GERSH, MARVIN J. *How to Raise Children at Home in Your Spare Time* Stein & Day, 1966

GINOTT, HAIM G. *Between Parent and Child* Macmillan, 1967

HARWOOD, A. C. *The Recovery of Man in Childhood* Hodder and Stoughton, 1958

HOLT, JOHN. *How Children Learn* Dell, 1971

HURLOCK, ELIZABETH B. *Child Development* McGraw-Hill, 1956

ILG, FRANCES L., and AMES, LOUISE BATES. *The Gesell Institute's Child Behavior* Barnes & Noble, 1972

KOCH, KENNETH. *Wishes, Lies and Dreams: Teaching Children to Write Poetry* Vintage, 1970

———— *Rose, Where Did You Get that Red?* Chelsea House/Random House, 1973

LANE, HOMER. *Talks to Parents and Teachers* Schocken, 1969

LEONARD, GEORGE B. *Education and Ecstasy* Dell, 1968

LÜSCHER, MAX. *The Lüscher Color Test* Pocket Books, 1971

LOPATE, PHILIP. *Being With Children* Doubleday, 1975

MONTESSORI, MARIA. *Dr. Montessori's Own Handbook* Schocken, 1970
—— *The Absorbent Mind* Delta, 1967
—— *The Child in the Family* Avon, 1972
NEILL, A. S. *Summerhill—A Radical Approach to Child Rearing* Hart, 1960
PIAGET, JEAN. *The Origins of Intelligence in the Child* Routledge, 1953
—— *The Child's Conception of Space* Humanities, 1956
PINES, MAYA. *Revolution in Learning* Harper, 1967
POMERANZ, VIRGINIA E. *The First Five Years* Doubleday, 1973
SMITH, CAM. *Buckminster Fuller to Children of Earth* Doubleday, 1972

SPOCK, BENJAMIN. *The Common Sense Book of Baby and Child Care* (First Edition) Duell, Sloan & Pearce, 1957
STANDING, E. M. *Maria Montessori—Her Life and Her Work* Mentor, 1962
—— *The Montessori Revolution in Education* Schocken Paperbacks, 1966
STEICHEN, EDWARD. *The Family of Man* for the Metropolitan Museum of Art Photographs, 1955
SUTTON, BRIAN, and SMITH, SHIRLEY. *How to Play with Your Children (And When Not To)* Hawthorne, 1975
WHITE, BURTON L. *The First Three Years of Life* Prentice-Hall, 1975

PAMPHLETS

Nursery School Settings Invitation to What? BEYER, EVELYN National Association for the Education of Young Children
Planning Environments for Young Children —Physical Space, KRITCHEVSKY, SYBIL; PRESCOTT, ELIZABETH; WALLING, LEE
The Celebration of Color Reprinted by courtesy of Lithopinion Purchase at Metropolitan Museum of Art

Water, Sand and Mud As Play Materials National Association for the Education of Young Children
What We Can Learn From Infants Proceedings of a Conference jointly sponsored by Yale Child Study Center, Yale University—National Association for the Education of Young Children

SHOPPING GUIDE

A few places mentioned are:

Childcraft Center, 150 East 58th Street, New York, N.Y. 10022

Children's Room, Inc. (The), 318 East 45th Street, New York, N.Y. 10017

Children's Workbench (The), 470 Park Avenue South, New York, N.Y. 10016

Community Playthings, Rifton, New York 12471

Creative Playthings, 1 East 53rd Street, New York, N.Y. 10022

Design Research, 53 East 57th Street, New York, N.Y. 10022 (Fabrics and Furniture)

Fabrications, 146 East 56th Street, New York, N.Y. 10022 (Fabrics only)

Loftcraft, 1021 Third Avenue, New York, N.Y. 10021

Herman Miller, Inc., 600 Madison Avenue, New York, N.Y. 10022 and Zeeland, Michigan 49464

Scandinavian Design, Inc., 117 East 59th Street, New York, N.Y. 10022